Federal Tax Treatment
of
State and Local Securities

Federal Tax Treatment

of

State and Local Securities

DAVID J. OTT AND ALLAN H. MELTZER

A background paper prepared for a conference of
experts held January 25-26, 1962, together with a
summary of the conference discussion

Studies of Government Finance

THE BROOKINGS INSTITUTION

WASHINGTON, D.C.

THE BROOKINGS INSTITUTION is an independent organization devoted to nonpartisan research, education, and publication in economics, government, foreign policy, and the social sciences generally. Its principal purposes are to aid in the development of sound public policies and to promote public understanding of issues of national importance.

The Institution was founded December 8, 1927, to merge the activities of the Institute for Government Research, founded in 1916, the Institute of Economics, founded in 1922, and the Robert Brookings Graduate School of Economics and Government, founded in 1924.

The general administration of the Institution is the responsibility of a self-perpetuating Board of Trustees. The Trustees are likewise charged with maintaining the independence of the staff and fostering the most favorable conditions for creative research and education. The immediate direction of the policies, program, and staff of the Institution is vested in the President, assisted by the division directors and an advisory council, chosen from the professional staff of the Institution.

In publishing a study, the Institution presents it as a competent treatment of a subject worthy of public consideration. The interpretations and conclusions in such publications are those of the author or authors and do not purport to represent the views of the other staff members, officers, or trustees of the Brookings Institution.

Foreword

This volume on the federal tax treatment of state and local government securities is the second Brookings publication of the series of Studies of Government Finance sponsored by the National Committee on Government Finance, and it is the first of this series stemming from the Conference Program of the National Committee. The volume includes a study undertaken by the authors in 1961 to provide background material for a conference of experts on the taxation of state and local securities, held at the Brookings Institution on January 25 and 26, 1962, together with a summary of the discussion at the conference.

The federal income tax exemption for state and local government securities has been a controversial issue for many years. Opponents of the exemption believe that it is inequitable, reduces risk investment by high-bracket taxpayers, and costs an excessive amount to the federal government. Proponents of the present treatment argue that elimination of the tax exemption would make the cost of borrowing to many state and local governments prohibitive. They believe that it would be unwise public policy to remove the tax exemption, in view of the mounting needs of these units of government. The purpose of the study by Professors David J. Ott and Allan H. Meltzer, and of the conference, was to try to narrow down the differences among experts in taxation and the municipal bond market on the facts and analyses with regard to this matter of public policy.

The conference was attended by thirty-four individuals representing various shades of opinion on the tax treatment of interest on state and local government securities. A list of the conferees is given on pages 127-28. The individuals were selected on the basis of their background, experience, and ability to contribute to a discussion of the technical issues in this field. The participants were invited in their personal capacities, and not as representatives of the firms, agencies, or institutions with which they are affiliated.

The conference revealed a sharp difference of opinion regarding the policy of tax exemption for interest paid on state and local government bonds. It was possible, nevertheless, to discuss the technical issues with profit. At this level, some progress was made toward creating a better understanding of the conflicting statements of fact and analysis often made by different groups and individuals. It is hoped that the study together with the conference summary will be as helpful to others in this respect as the conference was to the participants.

The original material in all of the chapters, except Chapter V, and the conference summary were prepared by Professor Ott. Professor Meltzer prepared Chapter VI and participated in the revision of the entire manuscript for publication. Many people assisted the authors at one point or another. They are especially grateful to the Advisory Committee, consisting of Raymond W. Goldsmith, Frank E. Morris, L. L. Ecker-Racz, and Roland I. Robinson; to Joseph A. Pechman, who planned and organized the project; and to George Conklin, C. J. Devine, Richard Goode, James O'Leary, Mortimer Kaplan, Warren L. Smith, and Norman Ture. Professor Smith greatly improved earlier results in the algebraic analysis in Chapter IV. Mrs. Shirley Lau and Miss Irene Lurie served as capable research assistants. Mrs. Catherine Mallardi typed the manuscript, and Miss Marcia Appel supervised the production of the manuscript in its several drafts and expurgated numerous errors of composition and form. Miss A. Evelyn Breck edited the manuscript, with the assistance of Mrs. Medora Richardson. Mrs. Virginia Haaga prepared the index.

The National Committee on Government Finance was established in 1960 by the trustees of the Brookings Institution to supervise a comprehensive program of studies on taxation and government expenditure. The program sponsored by the National Committee is supported with funds provided by the Ford Foundation.

The views expressed in this study are those of the authors and do not purport to represent the views of the National Committee on Government Finance or the staff members, officers, or trustees of the Brookings Institution.

ROBERT D. CALKINS
President

January 1963

Studies of Government Finance

Studies of Government Finance is a special program of research and education in taxation and government expenditures at the federal, state, and local levels. These studies are under the supervision of the National Committee on Government Finance appointed by the Trustees of the Brookings Institution, and are supported by a special grant from the Ford Foundation.

MEMBERS OF THE ADVISORY COMMITTEE

Contents

Text Tables

Charts

Appendix Tables

CHAPTER I

Introduction and Summary

INTEREST INCOME FROM SECURITIES issued by state and local governments was specifically exempted from the federal income tax under section 103(a)(1) of the first Income Tax Act passed pursuant to the Sixteenth Amendment. Virtually every Secretary of the Treasury since its passage has favored removing the exemption feature. Public finance experts have repeatedly attacked it, and volumes of testimony before congressional tax committees have been heard in connection with its repeal. Despite this rather concerted opposition, Congress has some six times defeated proposals to remove the exemption, and on many more occasions such proposals have never reached a vote.[1] The retention of the exemption feature in the face of such formidable opposition has reflected the efforts of countless state, municipal, county, and other elected and appointed officials, together with representatives of the financial houses underwriting and dealing in tax-exempt securities.

The issue, measured in dollar terms, is not small. Total interest payments of state and local governments in 1961 were over $2 billion on some $70 billion of state and local government debt out-

---

[1] Derrick lists some 114 resolutions that were introduced from 1920 through 1943 to repeal the exemptions (including that on U.S. bonds). Lucille Derrick, "Exemption of Security Interest from Income Taxes in the United States," *Journal of Business*, Vol. 19 (October 1946), Pt. 1, App.

standing.[2] In recent years, about 50 or 60 percent of construction outlays have been financed through issues of tax-exempt state-local securities.[3] Interest cost savings to state and local governments due to lower interest rates on their security issues, and the loss of revenue to the federal government due to the exempt status of such securities are somewhere within a range of $500-$1200 million. Precisely where shall concern us in considerable detail later. Pechman has estimated that in 1957 the exemption feature accounted for about 5 percent of personal income tax yield lost through exclusions of all types from adjusted gross income.[4] Hellmuth estimates that approximately the same proportion of exclusions from the corporate tax base is accounted for by tax-exempt interest.[5] No wonder the protagonists in the controversy have spoken out rather strongly; and that the accumulation of literature on the subject and the list of arguments and counter-arguments has grown to somewhat awesome proportions.

Recently, the issue has been before us again. The Ways and Means Committee of the House of Representatives devoted a part of its 1959 Hearings on Tax Revision to a discussion of this subject, and it seems likely that proposals to effect some changes in the tax treatment of interest on state-local bonds will continue to be forthcoming—to be debated and decided in the Congress again.

This study seeks to accomplish two things. First, the economic arguments put forth by previous writers will be summarized. In the entire literature on the subject, no single reference pulls together the main arguments which have been used, and a collation of these would seem useful as groundwork for further discussion. Second, some new material will be presented bearing on the most belabored points in the controversy: (1) "The" differential between yields on

[2] *Survey of Current Business* (July 1962). Debt figure is an average of 1960 and 1961 outstandings, from *Federal Reserve Bulletin*.

[3] See Roland I. Robinson, *The Postwar Market for State and Local Government Securities* (National Bureau of Economic Research, 1960), pp. 40-45. His data extend only through 1956. The same procedure was applied for 1956-61 to obtain the figure mentioned in the text. In brief, gross issues of state-local securities less issues used for refunding and veterans aid were compared with state-local construction outlays taken from the national income accounts.

[4] Joseph A. Pechman, "What Would a Comprehensive Individual Income Tax Yield?", House Committee on Ways and Means, *Tax Revision Compendium*, Vol. 1 (1959), p. 279.

[5] William F. Hellmuth, "The Corporate Income Tax Base," *ibid.*, p. 313.

taxable securities and tax-exempt securities; (2) the interest cost savings for the state and local governments versus the revenue foregone by the federal government; and (3) the problems of transition in case of removal of the exemption, with emphasis on alternative subsidies for state and local governments and the treatment of debt outstanding. The conclusions reached on these and other issues are summarized in the following sections.

The Issues

Chapter II summarizes the economic arguments made for and against the elimination of tax exemption. Four basic points are made by those who oppose the federal income tax exemption of state-local bond interest: (1) The exemption is inequitable because it discriminates among individuals in similar economic circumstances and principally benefits taxpayers in the highest income brackets. (2) Risk investment is reduced because potential investors are encouraged to purchase tax-exempts. (3) A misallocation of resources in the private sector and between the public and private sector results from the encouragement given to local government projects. (4) The subsidy is inefficient because, first, federal revenues are reduced more than interest costs to states and municipalities; second, the borrowing which is subsidized is not directly correlated with need; third, the least benefit is obtained by communities with the lowest credit rating.

Supporters of the exemption defend their views on the following grounds: (1) Interest costs of states and municipalities will rise "sharply" if the exemption is removed—more than the usual comparisons of yields of outstanding corporates and municipals would suggest. This argument is based on the view that municipals are not as attractive as corporates (and other securities) in terms of "marketability." (2) The nation's tax structure will become less progressive, or more regressive, as state-local taxes rise to finance capital outlays. (3) The understated rise in interest costs will prevent some local government units from borrowing. This will curtail necessary state-capital outlays. (4) Alternative subsidies will reduce the fiscal independence of the state and local governments and produce further centralization in government.

Further, the two sides disagree on the constitutionality issue, that is, on whether the federal government has the power to levy an income tax on interest payments paid by state and local governments. Since this study is limited to an appraisal of the economic issues, the constitutionality question is not discussed here.

The Yield Differential

New data and a new estimate of the yield differential between taxables and exempts are presented in Chapter III after a brief discussion of the determinants and trend of the differential. It is suggested there that the spread between exempt and taxable securities of comparable quality is related to the relative supply of tax-exempt securities, the tax rates applicable to the various tax brackets, the wealth position of asset-holders in each tax bracket, and preferences of investors for various types of securities. In the postwar period, the ratio of the differential to corporate yields (based on outstanding securities) has fallen. Also, the ratios for the highest and lowest rated securities have tended to equality, especially since 1956.

Quantitative evidence throws light on what yields on municipals would be without the exemption feature. A comparison of corporate and municipal yields during 1900-13, when neither type of interest was subject to income taxation, suggests that the yield on municipals without the exemption feature would not exceed corporate yields. The same conclusion is indicated by a comparison of Canadian municipal and corporate yields for recent years. However, the spread between reoffering yields on taxable Canadian municipal and provincial securities offered in United States markets and United States municipal yields is greater than differentials between United States corporates and municipals. This suggests a larger differential than the present spread between corporate and municipal yields. On the other hand, the experience with serials on railroad equipment trust obligations indicates that municipals will not sell at a discount because they are generally in serial form. Finally, yields on bond issues of religious institutions, which might be similar to those issued by small municipalities, suggest possible after-removal yields for municipals of from $5\frac{1}{2}$ to 6 percent in 1960.

A number of capital market experts were asked for their opinions on the yields of municipals if the exemption feature is removed. In general, these experts believe (1) that yields on municipals would rise by more than the current differential between new issue yields on municipals and public corporate bonds. This view is based on the assumption that private placement yields are the relevant ones at which the large institutional buyers would become active in the market for municipals if they were taxable. (2) They suggest that the municipal yield curve—that is, the curve relating yield to maturity and time to maturity—would have a much lower slope after removal of the exemption feature. This conclusion is based on the assumption that there would be increased institutional buying in the longer maturities and less institutional buying at the short-end. (3) The market experts generally agree that municipals would not sell at a discount because of the serial form of such issues.

A range for the yield differential on long-term bonds was computed in the light of the quantitative data and the views of the capital market specialists. For 1957-60, this range was 1.01-1.84 percentage points. The difference between yields on private corporate placements and yields on municipals of comparable quality was taken as a maximum; the minimum was set at the differential between public corporate new issue yields and municipal yields.

Estimating the effect of higher yields if the exemption is removed required that some account be taken of the "flattening" of the slope of the yield curve. In 1960 a complete flattening of the yield curve would have had the same effect on interest costs as a rise of 25 basis points in yields for all maturities. (One basis point is equal to one one-hundredth of a percentage point.) This is clearly a maximum since it implies that bond yields are independent of maturity. A generous allowance of 18 basis points was made for the flattening effect. This suggests a range of 1.19-2.02 percentage points as a measure of the rise in yield.

New Estimates of Interest Saved and Revenue Lost

Chapters IV and V restudy the interest cost—revenue lost problem on the assumption that yields in all maturities would be 1.19-2.02 percentage points higher. In this case, average annual interest payments on a stratified sample of 202 municipals issued in 1960 would have been 30.7-53.5 percent higher. Federal revenue from the taxation of interest on these issues would have to be 23.5-34.9 percent of the additional interest payments before the revenue gain would begin to exceed the value of the exemption on these issues.

The revenue obtained from removing tax exemption depends on the distribution of state and local government securities after removal and the tax rate schedule. At one extreme, assume that there is no change in the distribution of new municipal issues. This would occur if there were no alternative sources of tax-sheltered income desirable to those presently holding municipals. In this case, the revenue yield is obtained by using the average marginal tax rates applicable to present holders of municipal bonds. At the other extreme, the tax yield would be based on the average marginal tax rates of those who presently hold corporate securities. This occurs if present holders are able to shift to completely tax-free alternative sources of investment income and if taxable municipals are held in roughly the same proportions as corporates are held now.

On the basis of these extremes, federal revenues would be between 14 and 47 percent of post-removal interest payments. The maximum revenue is obtained by using the weighted average marginal tax rate applicable to present holders of municipal bonds, that is, assuming no shift in the distribution of new issues. The weighted average marginal tax rate of present holders of corporate issues sets the minimum tax yield for the Treasury. A realistic shift pattern gives a tax yield of 41-43 percent, suggesting that the revenue yield would be near the maximum end of the range. This follows from the fact that, at least in the short run, the distribution of security issues by type of issue remains relatively constant. Any attempt by present purchasers of tax-exempts to obtain tax shelters by acquiring alternative securities will be largely offset by the purchases of taxable state and local securities by former holders of the alternative securities.

Thus removal of the exemption would most likely produce more federal revenue than it would cost the states and municipalities. A precise numerical estimate has not been made. The future revenue gain depends on the volume and maturity distribution of future issues, interest rate differentials, yield curves, tax rate schedules, and other factors.

If the federal exemption for state and local securities is removed, it is likely that states would be permitted to tax interest on federal securities. Such taxes would have increased aggregate state revenues by $180 million in 1960, given the taxes now levied by states on personal and corporate incomes. Doubtless this is a minimum estimate, since some states might adopt income taxes or increase rates.

Outstanding State-Local Debt

If the exemption is removed from outstanding state-local securities, the revenue gain to the Treasury will reflect (1) the revenues received from taxing the interest on the outstanding bonds until they mature, (2) the yield from taxing capital gains at maturity, and (3) the loss of revenue from realized capital losses sustained when the exemption is removed. The present value of the algebraic sum of these three items is about $4.5-$5 billion. The Treasury would receive a net gain of receipts, in present value terms, from taxing outstandings. However, taxing the interest on outstanding issues complicates management of the federal debt; on balance those shifting into municipals will discard more long-term federal securities than those shifting out will acquire at present yields. Yields on federal government bonds will rise. Taxing outstandings tends to cause equity yields to fall slightly and produces a sharp decline in commercial bank earnings. These estimates of the revenue gain and attendant capital market changes are discussed in Chapter VI.

If the federal tax exemption is removed, inequities arise whether the tax applies to new issues only or to new issues and outstandings. In the former case, present holders obtain windfalls as the value of their securities increases in response to the shrinking supply; in the latter case, they suffer capital losses. Methods have been devised to avoid such capital losses if outstanding issues are taxed. However, the inequities, compliance, and administrative problems are fewer if the exemption is removed from new issues only.

State Distribution of Exemption Benefits
and Alternative Subsidies

A state-by-state comparison of per-capita state-local debt and per-capita personal income indicates that borrowing is apparently inversely related to income level. Average credit quality of securities for the various states does not seem to be related—either directly or inversely—to average income. Thus, we have found no evidence that the subsidy from the tax exemption is distributed in accordance with "need" in any meaningful sense.

The distribution of benefits from exemption and numerous alternatives to tax exemption are discussed in Chapter VII. Among proposed alternatives considered are: Federal payments of some fixed proportion of the interest costs on new borrowing; tax credits calculated to equal the value of the exemption for the marginal investor in municipals; federal and state-local sharing of the additional revenues; creation of semiofficial or official intermediaries to lend money to state and local governments at low interest rates; grants for state-local capital outlays; and grants without any limitations on the use of the funds. Most of these suggestions are judged to be administratively feasible.

CHAPTER II

The Issues

PROPOSALS TO REMOVE the tax exemption feature have stimulated substantial discussion. This chapter first presents the economic arguments of those who favor removing tax exemption. Then arguments and rebuttal of those favoring retention of the present treatment are discussed. No position is taken here with respect to the validity of these arguments. Some are dealt with separately in later chapters.

Arguments for Removing the Exemption

Equity Considerations

The dominant argument against the present tax treatment of state and local government securities has been that it violates generally accepted principles of equity in taxation. In this view, an income tax should apply equally to equal incomes, and there should be some measure of progressivity—those with higher incomes should have greater proportionate tax burdens. It might be argued that on the first count no equity issue exists, since by accepting a lower yield on tax-exempt securities, investors give up income equivalent to the income tax obligation that would arise if they invested in fully taxable securities. This is true only of the marginal investor for whom the yield differential between exempts and taxables is equal to the marginal tax rate.

For the intramarginal bondholders subject to much higher marginal tax rates, there are substantial tax savings, varying with the level of income and marginal tax rate of the particular investor. For example, if the yield on fully taxable bonds is 3 percent and that on comparable tax-exempts is 2.1 percent, there is no tax saving for the marginal investor in the 30 percent tax bracket. Investment in taxables yields a return which, when taxed at the marginal rate. results in an after-tax yield of 2.1 percent. However, for the investor in, say, the 91 percent tax bracket, a substantial tax-saving results from investment in tax-exempts. If he buys fully taxable securities, the effective after tax yield is but 0.27 percent, as compared to 2.1 percent received from holding tax-exempts. Clearly, the exemption feature produces horizontal inequities, except for the income bracket indicated as marginal by yield differentials.[1]

In addition, the tax obviously reduces the progressivity of the income tax to the extent that those subject to high tax rates avail themselves of the exemption feature. This does not imply that high income recipients will seek to convert all their assets to state and local government securities and restrict their incomes to interest on these securities. Recent developments in the theory of portfolio composition suggest that, even in the highest income and wealth brackets, a considerable measure of portfolio diversification is to be expected.[2] Investors can be expected to compare risk of default and capital loss with the return on each asset. The proportion of any asset in their total portfolio will reflect their judgment of the equality of the marginal rate of substitution and the market terms of exchange between risk and return (where the risk attached to an additional unit of any asset rises with the proportion of assets held in that form).

In the absence of substantial risk aversion by high-income recipients, the proportion of assets held in the form of state and local government securities should be greatest in the top tax brackets. This is so because the marginal after-tax return per dollar invested

[1] If tax rates were not progressive and wealth and income were perfectly correlated, there would be no issue of horizontal equity, assuming the market discounted the value of the exemption precisely. There would still, of course, be resource reallocation effects which might be undesirable.

[2] See James M. Tobin, "Liquidity Preference as Behavior Towards Risk," *Review of Economic Studies*, Vol. 25 (October 1958), and Harry Markowitz, *Portfolio Composition* (John Wiley & Sons, 1959).

increases with taxable income. Estate tax data support this implication amply—the proportion of assets held in the form of state and local government securities rises with the size of estate.[3] And it seems reasonable to assume a close correlation between average lifetime income and size of estate.

Other evidence also suggests that upper income and wealth groups avail themselves of this opportunity to reduce their taxes. Lent found that two-thirds of the state and local government securities held by individuals were held by the upper one percent income group.[4] Similar results were obtained by Atkinson.[5] Using estate tax data, Mendershausen found that, in 1944, 90 percent of state and local government securities were held by individuals for whom an estate tax return would have been mandatory if they had died in that year.[6] Lampman computed a figure in excess of 100 percent for 1953,[7] indicating some problem in the estimating technique but suggestive of a high actual figure. In short, available data indicate that ownership of state and local government securities by individuals is concentrated in the upper income groups, and that some reduction in the progressivity of the federal income tax occurs as a result of the exemption feature.

Effect on Resource Allocation
in the Private Sector

RISK INVESTMENT. Some analysts have attacked the exemption on the ground that it withdraws risk or venture capital from the private sector which would otherwise be invested in productive enter-

[3] See data presented by Cushman McGee, "Exemption of Interest on State and Municipal Bonds," House Committee on Ways and Means, *Tax Revision Compendium*, Vol. 1 (1959), p. 765. Cited hereafter as *Compendium*.

[4] George E. Lent, *The Ownership of Tax-Exempt Securities, 1913-1953*, National Bureau of Economic Research, Occasional Paper 47 (1953), p. 116.

[5] Thomas R. Atkinson, *The Pattern of Financial Asset Ownership: Wisconsin Individuals, 1949* (National Bureau of Economic Research, 1956). See App. Table A-3.

[6] Horst Mendershausen, "The Pattern of Estate Tax Wealth," in Raymond Goldsmith, Dorothy S. Brady, and Horst Mendershausen, *A Study of Savings in the United States* (National Bureau of Economic Research, 1955), Vol. 3, p. 361.

[7] Robert J. Lampman, *Changes in the Share of Wealth Held by Top Wealth-Holders, 1922-1956*, National Bureau of Economic Research, Occasional Paper 71 (1960), p. 26. The 1958 estate tax return data suggest a figure of about 85 percent, according to some preliminary and unpublished work by Raymond Goldsmith. It is likely that the 1953 data were distorted by one or two unusual estates.

prise. Other observers have suggested that risk capital flows mainly from investors in the higher income brackets. It seems likely that the high effective after-tax yield of tax-exempts increases investor demand for state-local securities. Whether or not this diversion of capital from the private to the public sector will come mainly at the expense of private risk capital is, however, another question. It has been argued that if wealthy persons can put part of their portfolios in tax-exempts, thereby assuring themselves of reasonably safe income, they may be more willing to risk the remainder. Thus, the income security and after-tax yields of tax-exempts may increase risk investment.[8]

During the period in which the exemption feature has been in effect, any tendency for exemption to reduce the flow of risk capital has been obscured by the tax treatment of capital gains. To the extent that the lower rates on long-term capital gains have raised the after-tax yields on common stock investments, risk-taking has been encouraged. How much tax exemption has reduced risk investment in the private sector is difficult to ascertain or to separate from other economic, political, and legal changes.

USE OF FUNDS TO COMPETE WITH AND AID PRIVATE INDUSTRY. To some extent, funds obtained by state and local governments have been used to engage in what may be called business enterprises, for example, public utilities, housing developments and in some cases subsidies encouraging the growth of local industry. To the extent that these uses are encouraged, the exemption distorts the pattern of resource use. Resources are diverted to provide more (or less) of certain goods and services than would have occurred otherwise. In such cases the value of the marginal product of the capital employed is below its opportunity cost, resulting in a misallocation of resources. In the provision of these services, there is

---

[8] This point is made by Lyle C. Fitch, *Taxing Municipal Bond Income* (University of California Press, 1950), p. 49. This argument is weakened, however, to the extent that safe income is available in both taxable and tax sheltered form (that is, oil production royalties in proven fields). Furthermore, as J. Keith Butters, Lawrence E. Thompson, and Lynn L. Bollinger found in their study, *Effects of Taxation: Investments by Individuals* (Harvard University Business School, 1953), p. 287, those who hold a relatively large portion of their portfolios in tax-exempts are not aggressive in their allocation of the rest of their portfolios.

an increase in the capital stock that would not occur without the exemption feature.

A particular manifestation of the use of proceeds from state and local government security issues to alter resource allocation is the so-called industrial development bond. These bonds are issued by municipalities, generally in the South, and are used to build tax-exempt facilities for firms which lease the facilities from the municipality. The bonds are a liability of the issuing authority, not of the firm that obtains the facility. The imprimatur of the municipality is used to obtain low interest rates for a private concern—the concern benefiting from correspondingly lower rental payments (and higher profits) on the facility.

Several objections to the tax-exempt status of municipal industrial development bonds have been raised.[9] First, it is asserted that the bonds are a perversion of the basis on which the exemption feature rests—the public purpose of the municipal government function. Second, their primary use in getting industry and payrolls into an area has too often been at the expense of other areas. In some cases areas of substantial unemployment lose industry. The resource shift might not have occurred without the tax and leasing costs advantage. Third, they constitute a threat to the financial stability of the issuing government. Finally, this form of exemption results in discriminatory taxation at both federal and local levels— at the federal level because of the tax exemption for the interest paid and at the local level because the facility constructed is usually exempt from local property taxes.

This is one area where the protagonists have shown a degree of agreement. Generally, observers have condemned the use of industrial development bonds, whether or not they otherwise favor the interest exemption feature. However, attempts to eliminate the exemption feature on such issues, or to make rental on such facilities not deductible as a business expense for income tax purposes, have failed. Apparently, at least some of the opposition which defeated these proposals came from supporters of the general exemption feature who felt that any change in the existing status of tax exemp-

[9] See Solomon Barkin, "Exclusion from Taxable Income of Interest on Municipal Bonds to Subsidize Industry Should be Discontinued," *Compendium*, pp. 729-35. The use of these bonds has not been large relative to total gross issues.

tion might be the opening wedge in removing the general exemption.

Effect on Resource Allocation Between
Public and Private Sector

During the early 1920's, the general business community joined with many economists and Secretary of the Treasury Mellon in assaulting the exemption feature. Some large part of this support came from private utilities fighting against the growth of municipally owned utilities. They maintained that the lower yields available to state and local governments encouraged "uneconomic" borrowing and misallocated resources from the private to the public sector. Loose versions of this argument charged that state and local governments engaged in "wasteful" and unnecessary projects, leading toward more socialism, under the stimulus of lower borrowing costs.[10] This particular argument has not received much attention in recent years.

Inefficiency of Exemption Feature as a Subsidy

Those attacking the exemption feature have generally recognized that state and local governments benefit from the premium attached by the market to the exemption privilege in the form of lower interest. However, they cite empirical studies showing (with one or two exceptions)[11] that the interest cost saving is much less than the revenue foregone by the federal government (see Table 1). In its most general form, this argument points out that among the possible devices for accomplishing the same goal—assisting or subsidizing capital outlays by state and local government—the exemption of bond interest from taxation does not have the lowest cost.

[10] For a summary of these arguments, see Lucille Derrick, "Exemption of Security Interest from Income Taxes in the United States: An Economic and Statistical Analysis," *Journal of Business*, Vol. 19, Pt. 2 (October 1946), pp. 18-22.

[11] C. O. Hardy and H. L. Lutz both found that the interest cost saving was at least as great (or greater in Lutz' study) as the revenue lost. See C. O. Hardy, *Tax-Exempt Securities and the Surtax* (Brookings Institution, 1926), Chap. 4, and H. L. Lutz, *The Fiscal and Economic Effects of the Taxation of Public Securities*, A Report prepared for the Comptroller of the State of New York, reprinted in *Taxation of Governmental Securities and Salaries*, Hearings before the Senate Special Committee on Taxation of Governmental Securities and Salaries, 76 Cong. 1 sess. (1939), pp. 91-186.

TABLE 1. Estimates of Interest Saving to State and Local Governments and Revenue Loss to Federal Government as Result of Tax Exemption

(Dollar amounts in millions)

Year	Revenue Loss	Interest Savings	Ratio of Column (2) to Column (1)	Investigator
	(1)	(2)	(3)	(4)
1939	$107–198	$ 40–105	0.37–.53%	Treasury
1942	184	120[a]	0.65	Treasury
1947	—[b]	—[b]	0.58	Robinson
1948	—[b]	—[b]	0.32	Robinson
1949	—[b]	—[b]	0.43	Robinson
1950	—[b]	—[b]	0.53	Robinson
1951	—[b]	—[b]	0.56	Robinson
1952	300	—	—	Surrey & Warren
	—[b]	—[b]	0.42	Robinson
1953	—[b]	—[b]	0.23	Robinson
1954	—[b]	—[b]	0.28	Robinson
1955	550–680	200–210	0.36–.31	Maxwell
	—[b]	—[b]	0.27	Robinson
1958	600	400	0.67	Kirby
	800	400	0.50	Brazer

Sources:
1939: *Taxation of Governmental Securities and Salaries*, Hearings before the Senate Special Committee on Taxation of Governmental Securities and Salaries, 76 Cong. 1 sess., pp. 10, 35.
1942: *Revenue Revision of 1942*, Hearings before the House Committee on Ways and Means, 77 Cong. 2 sess., Vol. 3, pp. 3079 ff.
1947-51, 1953-54: Roland I. Robinson, *The Postwar Market for State and Local Government Securities* (National Bureau of Economic Research, 1960), pp. 194–95
1952: Stanley S. Surrey and William C. Warren (eds.), *Federal Income Taxation, Cases and Materials, 1953–1955*, (Foundation Press, 1953–55), p. 166; Robinson, op. cit.
1955: James A. Maxwell, "Exclusion from Income of Interest on State and Local Government Obligations," House Committee on Ways and Means, *Tax Revision Compendium*, Vol. I (1959); Robinson, op. cit.
1958: Vance N. Kirby, "State and Local Bond Interest," *Compendium*; Harvey E. Brazer, "Interest on State and Local Bonds and the Federal Income Tax," *Compendium*.
[a] Not actually computed in source, but inferred from yield differential.
[b] Ratio computed from *incremental* data. Since these are not comparable to the others they are not shown here.

A marginal investor faced with a choice between a taxable and tax-exempt bond will choose the tax-exempt if, and only if, the after-tax yield on the taxable bond is no more than the tax-exempt yield. Given rising marginal tax rates, it is easy to construct examples which show that the investors subject to high marginal tax rates will receive a rate of return from tax-exempts that is higher than the after-tax yield on a bond with interest subject to tax. Since the market yield on tax-exempt bonds will be set by the marginal investor, the subsidy will cost more to the Treasury than the states and municipalities will gain in lower interest cost.

Indeed, together with the equity considerations mentioned previously, the charge of inefficiency has been the most forceful and impressive point on which the opponents of exemption have rested their case. Since the approaches used in the empirical studies have other important implications (for example, they imply the yields which would exist in the absence of exemption and thus suggest the rise in interest cost after removal) some detailed attention will be devoted to this argument in Chapters III, IV, and V.

Another variant of the charge of inefficiency against the exemption feature is that the benefits go largely to the less needy governmental units. Since the basis point differential has been greater between yields on the better grades of tax-exempts and corporate bonds,[12] the interest cost saving has not necessarily gone to those units with lowest income. Bonds issued by a large proportion of the smaller, less affluent governmental units are in the lower credit ratings or are unrated. The interest cost saving to the small units of government is much less relative to costs on comparable taxable issues than for the larger, wealthier cities or states. This is not caused by smallness per se, but because smaller government units often issue low-rated or unrated securities. However, the correlation is not perfect. There are small borrowing units with good credit ratings, and there are large borrowing units in the lower credit categories.

This point of inefficiency in the distribution of the subsidy has been put another way. To the extent that high income units—or units with rapidly growing incomes—tend to issue more debt, the subsidy appears to benefit those units and areas which are relatively less in "need."

Finally, some have questioned whether a subsidy tied to borrowing is preferable to a general subsidy of the capital expenditures for which most borrowing is undertaken. Although borrowing is closely related to capital expenditures, the data show also that per-

[12] This was pointed out by Robinson for the postwar period up to 1956. See Roland I. Robinson, *The Postwar Market for State and Local Government Securities* (National Bureau of Economic Research, 1960), pp. 173-80. This version of the inefficiency argument is most clearly stated by James A. Maxwell, "Exclusion from Income of Interest on State and Local Government Obligations, *Compendium*, p. 715.

haps 30 percent of state and local government capital expenditures are currently financed. The interest cost saving penalizes those communities which pay for their capital facilities and structures out of current taxes.[13]

Arguments for Retaining Present Treatment

The Constitutionality Question

Only brief mention has been made of the question of the constitutionality of taxing interest income from state and local government securities, although this alone has probably been discussed as much as all of the economic arguments combined. Those favoring retention of the exemption feature have laid great stress on legal opinions indicating that a statute to this effect would be unconstitutional.[14]

In this study, no attempt is made to pursue this point. The issue cannot be finally settled until the United States Supreme Court has had the opportunity to hand down a ruling. Whatever the answer, its main significance in the present context is in regard to the form any proposed elimination of the exemption feature would have to take. If the Sixteenth Amendment allows such taxation, a statute will suffice; if it does not, a constitutional amendment will have to be passed by the Congress and ratified by the necessary number of states. This does not mean, however, that the issues involved in the constitutionality question are unimportant. The separation of powers and the maintenance of fiscal independence with or without the exemption feature are rightly of concern. However, it seems likely that if Congress otherwise is willing to eliminate exemption, it would not be deterred by the prospect of having the law tested in the courts.

Interest Cost

By far the most common economic argument raised against elimination of the tax exemption for interest on state and local government securities is that doing so will bring about a "sharp"

---

[13] Robinson, *op. cit.*, p. 40. See also Goldsmith, *op. cit.*, Vol. 1, Tables, 6, 4, and 15. However, if there is local option in voting bond issues, there is a choice of debt or current income financing.

[14] See *inter alia*, McGee, *Compendium*, pp. 737-41.

rise in the interest costs of state and local governments. This one proposition is the starting point for the arguments made by those favoring retention, so it deserves special scrutiny.

No one denies that interest costs will rise. The disagreement relates to the adjective "sharp." In the first place, those favoring retention of the exemption feature argue that measures used by its critics understate the relevant yield differential between tax-exempts and corporate bonds. The relevant differential is that between new issue yields on comparable quality corporates and "municipals," whereas critics have generally used yields on outstandings. New issue yields on corporates are usually above yields on corporates outstanding, but this is not true in the case of tax-exempts. The differential between new issue yields on corporates and tax-exempts is greater, therefore, than that between yields on outstanding corporates and tax-exempts.[15]

Beyond this, however, those favoring the retention of the exemption feature believe (as do others) that yields on state and local government securities will rise by even more than the differential between new issue yields on tax-exempts and corporate bonds. The first reason advanced by proponents of exemption is that state and local government securities must yield more than corporates of comparable quality to compensate holders for their relative lack of "marketability." The term "marketability" is common in capital market vocabularies, but its meaning is not always made explicit.[16] As used in the present context, "marketability" seems to refer to the "depth" and "breadth" of the market for a security—that is, to the volume of transactions expected at or near the going market price and to the level of transactions costs, explicit or implicit, which tend to make sales more or less difficult and the security

[15] The average differential between yields on outstanding corporates and tax-exempts for the period 1957-60 was 94 basis points for Aaa-rated and 77 for Baa-rated bonds. On the other hand, the average differential between yields on newly issued corporate and tax-exempt securities was 144 basis points for those rated Aaa and 117 for Baa rated. Comparison of newly issued yield differentials for this period suggests, then, a greater yield differential of from 50 basis points for high-grade securities to 40 basis points for low-grade securities. Using the yield differential on new issues as the value of the exemption, higher interest costs of from 30 to 47 percent on the average would have been incurred during this period on the issues of rated state and local government securities; whereas, a like figure drawn from the yield differential on outstandings would be from 19 to 30 percent.

[16] See discussion in Robinson, *op. cit.*, pp. 153-55.

more or less liquid. Observers catalogue a number of characteristics of state and local government securities which produce
narrow and thin markets on the demand side. In effect these characteristics suggest a liquidity discount. They include:

1. The small size of many issues of state and local government
securities, which makes them unattractive to large institutional
buyers. Bond issues of small units of local government are relatively
small in total and most often issued in serial form. Each serial is
in effect a separate issue. No unique figure for the smallest-sized
issue that would attract large institutional buyers has been stated,
but certainly issues of $100,000 or less would attract little interest
from large institutional investors in the absence of a handling
charge or premium.[17]

2. The lack of information concerning many issues, particularly
smaller ones, makes these securities less marketable relative to
others. Although the rating services publish information on a large
number of issuing authorities, the coverage is far from complete.
One of the three large investment advisory services does not rate
issues of borrowing units where debt outstanding is less than
$600,000. Another sets its limit at $1 million.[18] The fact that there
is no "SEC" for such issues does not increase confidence in the information that is available. Issues which are unrated by investment
advisory services frequently have restricted sales to local buyers.
In recent years, some 60 percent of the number of new issues have
been unrated, although such issues accounted for only some 20 percent of the total dollar volume.[19]

---

[17] The median size issue of municipals is about $250,000 and has an average of 18
separate maturities. (Frank F. Morris, "Size Characteristics of Municipal Bond Issues,"
IBA Statistical Bulletin, January 1957, p. 1, and letter to authors.)

In an unpublished paper, Avery Cohan tested the effect of size of issue on offering
yield for publicly issued corporate bonds, on the stated ground that size of issue affects
"marketability" and thus yields. He found that out of 24 regressions (1 for issues in
each of 24 years during the period 1935-58) the regression coefficient for size of issues
was significant at the .90 level in only two cases. It is possible that the coefficient would
have been significant in more cases at some (slightly) lower level of confidence, but his
data are not presented in a way which allows us to check this. The lack of a strong
relation may reflect the fact that almost all small issues sold in recent years are
"sweetened" with warrants. See Avery Cohan, "Yields on New Underwritten Corporate Bonds." (Unpublished paper, University of North Carolina.)

[18] Cf. McGee, *Compendium,* pp. 755-56.

[19] *IBA Statistical Bulletin* (August 1959), p. 3.

Along this same line, observers have often noted special characteristics of competitive securities which raise their "marketability" relative to tax-exempts.[20] United States Government securities are: issued in multiple denominations from $50.00 up, interchangeable without cost; accepted as security for public deposits of the United States; accepted in numerous cases at par in payment of federal estate taxes, even though acquired at a discount; telegraphically transferable in amounts of $5,000 or more at a charge of not more than $10.00, by Federal Reserve Banks; eligible for open-market purchases by the Federal Reserve; eligible for use as collateral by fiduciaries acting under federal law; eligible as security for advances made to member banks by Federal Reserve Banks; and classified by bank examiners as "riskless assets." For corporate bonds and stock, proponents of continued exemption argue that investment managers of financial institutions are often personally acquainted with managements of various corporations and can readily evaluate their ability. They are accustomed to analyzing corporate financial statements but not those of state and local governments. Finally, these observers point out that corporate stocks have achieved a wider and deeper market due to the threat of inflation, the possibility of appreciation in market value, and the tax advantages attendant on capital gains.[21]

On these grounds then, the supporters of tax exemption argue that interest costs would rise sharply in the absence of the exemption. From this they draw several conclusions.

First, institutional and legal constraints would prevent the marketing of some issues at the higher yield levels. Many states and localities have statutes or constitutional provisions which set interest rate ceilings.[22]

Second, aside from the effect of institutional restraints, the higher level of interest rates would produce some combination of a reduced quantity of capital outlays and higher capital prices (costs)

[20] McGee, *Compendium*, pp. 744-48. It should be noted that the characteristics listed as raising the marketability of U.S. Government securities relative to state-local bonds are mostly not characteristic of corporates and should not affect "the" corporate versus state-local differential.

[21] *Ibid.*

[22] See Dick Netzer, "State-Local Response to Changing Credit Conditions: The Institutional Obstacles," *Journal of Finance*, Vol. 15 (May 1960), esp. pp. 224-26.

depending on the elasticity of demand for the services financed with borrowing. At one extreme, if the demand for the capital goods financed by borrowing is perfectly price inelastic, the result would be the same quantity of capital formation with higher prices per unit and greater total outlays. At the other extreme, where the demand for such capital projects is perfectly elastic at current prices, quantity would fall as well as total outlays. It is likely that the demand curve for many of these capital projects would be quite inelastic—there would probably be some quantity reduction but a much greater proportionate rise in price and an increase in total outlays. In short, aside from the interest rate ceiling barrier, it is claimed that a rise in the supply price of capital to these units would likely produce some restriction in capital formation but greater total dollar outlays. To the extent that capital formation is reduced, public facilities are not provided.

Third, if total outlays do rise, then state and local taxes must ultimately rise to service the increase in interest charges. This, it is argued, will increase the regressivity of the total tax structure. A reduction of the quantity of social capital provided will also have regressive effects, since, it is argued, the benefit from such services varies inversely with income.

Finally, the additional burden on state and local governments, together with such unmet requirements as for schools and roads, will intensify pressure for federal aid. Any such aid given to replace the lost interest cost savings will reduce the fiscal independence of states and their political subdivisions. This will lead to greater federal control and participation in the affairs of local governments.

The last point receives particular emphasis from those favoring retention of the exemption. Judging from the literature, it appears that this is the most basic fear that moves them to argue against repeal. They maintain that all the arguments about inefficiency and equity, even if accepted, are not strong enough to justify the increased control which they feel would surely accompany any alternative form of subsidy. For example, a pamphlet published by the Marine Trust Company of Western New York stated:

The immunity of interest on state and municipal bonds from federal income tax is essential to preserve the independent sovereignty of state and local governments under our dual state-federal system of government. *Any tax inequities in the federal tax system which may result from this immunity are trivial matters when weighted against the importance of preserving the independence of state and local governments.*[23]

The appeal of the exemption as a subsidy is that it is automatic, dispensed not by annual congressional decisions but by the impersonal forces of the capital markets. Those favoring exemption strongly feel that no alternative can match this attribute. Even if there were no administrative controls over an alternative subsidy, it would still depend on annual or periodic support from Congress and the Executive. This would open numerous opportunities to have increased surveillance and control of the subsidy tacked on in years when those favoring increased federal power or responsibility have political strength.

This is a point on which economic analysis can have little to say, yet it is a legitimate point. Optimum allocation of resources and equity considerations are not the only standards on which policy decisions are made. Various proposed alternative subsidies are presented in Chapter VII. But no attempt is made to evaluate how much control or supervision would result under these alternative subsidies or whether the automatic yield effect of the present exemption feature can be approximated in some other way.

Unrated Issues

Heavy emphasis is placed by those favoring retention of the present treatment on the asserted plight of smaller borrowing units, in particular those with lower credit ratings or those whose issues are unrated. The current market for state and locals is at least a dual one. One part consists of a large, broad, national market for large issues. The other is a series of separate local markets for the smaller, usually unrated, issues. In the event of removal of the exemption feature, it is adjudged that the units borrowing in the national market will continue to have little difficulty in placing their issues though they will pay "substantially higher" interest costs.

[23] *Tax Exemption: A Discussion of the Immunity of Interest on Bonds of States and Municipalities from Federal Income Tax* (May 1961). Italics added.

For the issues of small governments, however, it is maintained that a serious marketing problem would arise. These units typically place their issues with local buyers—in particular local banks and wealthier individuals. Adherents of the present system allege that this demand source would "dry up" if the exemption is eliminated. Moreover, they assert that there would be few new buyers of major importance interested in the small, local issues. This is a difficult judgment to evaluate. It does seem a priori unlikely that insurance companies, pension funds, and mutual savings banks would evince any interest in the small, unrated issues, except at increased relative yields because of the small size and high transactions costs on these issues and because of the lack of adequate information. It should be noted, however, that many institutional investors deal heavily in small residential mortgages and that local or regional tax laws give certain tax advantages to investors in state and local government issues.[24] Furthermore, it could be expected that some of the smaller mutual savings banks might give some support to issues in the New England region.

On the other hand, it is argued that the exemption feature at present offers relatively less aid to the large number of small governments which issue unrated or low rated bonds than to those in higher quality classes, as pointed out earlier. Any attempt to remove the exemption feature, however, must carefully consider the problem of marketing the issues of small, unrated borrowers. It will be discussed again in Chapter III.

[24] Under Texas insurance laws, for example, "foreign" life, health, and accident insurance companies are taxed on their gross premiums (less refunds and dividends) under a sliding scale. The rate is lower the greater the proportion of investments in "Texas securities" (bonds of Texas governmental units, mortgages on Texas land, and a few others). See "Statutory Background of Texas Taxes," unpublished paper by Alan R. Bromberg, Southern Methodist University Law School. Pennsylvania exempts from personal property tax the securities of local government units within the state. Numerous similar examples can be found.

CHAPTER III

Yield Differential on Taxable
and Tax-Exempt Securities

WHAT WOULD YIELDS on tax-exempts be without the exemption feature? In this chapter this much discussed question is reopened. First, some theory of the determination of the yield differential is introduced, and the trend of the differential since 1946 is summarized. Then some quantitative evidence which throws light on the differential is presented. Finally, the opinions of several capital market experts are summarized and used together with the quantitative evidence to obtain an estimated range for the likely, current yield differential.

Factors Affecting "the" Yield Differential

Two factors which affect the yield differential between taxable securities and tax-exempt securities are: (1) the value of the exemption to marginal investors; and (2) differences in risk attached to tax-exempt and taxable securities.

It is difficult to reach a conclusion about the importance of the second of these factors. The same rating scales are used to rate both types of issues, but the criteria employed to assign ratings differ substantially. Thus an A rated municipal may be of better or worse quality than a similarly rated corporate. Some believe that tax-exempts, particularly general revenue obligations, are of higher quality than comparably rated taxable issues. In support of this position, it is often argued that general revenue tax-exempts are supported by taxing power, that there have been few defaults that have not been discharged eventually by payment in full, and that the long-term record of municipal credit has been very good. Others point out that the dangers of "fiscal irresponsibility," of the "wrong crowd" taking political power, of political rather than business management, and similar vaguely defined dangers are more relevant to municipal bonds than to corporates. Most analysts agree that the default risk has been lower for municipal bonds. But they point to political dangers and the economic problems posed by "one industry towns" that lose their major revenue sources as suggestive of the factors increasing the risk of receiving coupon payments when due.

Regarding the value of the exemption to marginal investors, differences in credit quality are probably a small factor in explaining differences in yields on similarly rated bonds. In the following discussion, we shall assume that such differences can be ignored and that the differential in interest rates paid on municipal and corporate bonds depends on the marginal tax rate applicable to the marginal investor.

Suppose we have the following schedule of marginal rates for investors:

Taxable Income	Marginal Tax Rate
Over $150,000	90%
$50,000–$149,999	60
25,000– 49,999	40
10,000– 24,999	30
Less than 10,000	20

The relative return on investment at the margin on a taxable security yielding X percent or a tax-exempt security of comparable risk yielding 0.10X percent would be a matter of indifference to an investor with income of $150,000 or more. Both offer the same after-tax marginal return. Given his assets and tastes, an investor will hold increasing amounts of tax-exempt securities as the ratio of yield on tax-exempts to yield on taxables (r_e/r_t) rises above 0.1.

For as r_e/r_t rises, after-tax return on tax-exempts rises relative to the return on taxables. Similar behavior would follow for others in this bracket. At any r_e/r_t there exists a quantity of tax-exempt securities demanded by investors in this bracket.

Investors in the next lower tax bracket, however, will not consider tax-exempts until the r_e/r_t ratio reaches 0.4. At this point the after-tax yield to them on taxables is the same as on tax-exempts. Given their assets and tastes, there will be an increasing amount of tax-exempts demanded by them as r_e/r_t rises above 0.4. Again, given their wealth position and preferences, the amount of tax-exempt securities they will want to hold will increase with the ratio r_e/r_t. The same procedure applies to investors in lower tax brackets.

In the discussion which follows, we assume that the market yields of bonds depend on the available stock of bonds—that is, that stocks are large relative to flows. Further, we assume for the present that there is a given stock of taxable bonds. The equilibrium ratio r_e/r_t will be set where the stock of state and local bonds outstanding is equal to the amount which investors in all tax brackets desire to hold. This is shown in the following figure illustrating the supply and demand situation for funds in the market for state and local government securities. Investors in the \$150,000+ bracket will hold an amount of bonds (supply money) at each ratio of tax-exempt yields to taxable yields (r_e/r_t) as shown by S_1; investors in the \$50,000-\$100,000 bracket will supply funds at each relative yield in amounts shown by S_2. S_3, S_4, and S_5 show the amount supplied by those in lower tax brackets. The horizontal summation of these supply curves is ΣS, the aggregate supply curve of funds (demand to hold bonds) in the state and local government market at various relative yields.

By assumption, the stock of bonds issued by state and local governments is fixed. Then the market is cleared at relative yield $OM = 0.7$. The upper bracket holds OB of bonds, the next lower bracket OA, and the next lower, OC. For any ΣS, a new issue of bonds by state and local governments will affect the equilibrium relative yields and would appear as an increase in DD. This would increase the ratio r_e/r_t. Any decrease in DD, for example, a net reduction in the stock of state and local governments, will lower the ratio.

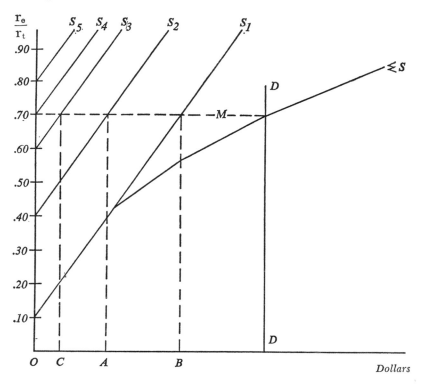

Changes in the tax rates applicable to the brackets will affect each S curve and the equilibrium ratio, *ceteris paribus*. Increases in the marginal tax rates (or expected rates) shift each S curve and the ΣS curve to the right. This would produce a lower equilibrium r_e/r_t and conversely. In addition, changes in the tastes of investors, given their assets, would affect their planned purchases of state and local government securities. Finally, changes in wealth affect the S curves and ΣS; an increase in wealth shifts the S curves to the right; decreases in wealth shift the curve to the left.

In short, given the total stock of all securities, the relative yield reflects: (1) the stock of tax-exempt securities; (2) the tax rates applicable to each bracket; (3) the wealth position of individuals in each income bracket; and (4) tastes.

Obviously, a statistical attempt to fit the relative differential to these variables faces formidable obstacles. Continuous data are lacking on assets by tax brackets; the market yield in fact depends on the interaction of stocks and flows. While marginal tax rates for each bracket and ex-post data on the amount of new issues are available, knowledge of sales and acquisition by income or wealth classes are lacking. Derrick[1] sought to explain the relative differential for 1919-41, using as independent variables a weighted average of supramarginal tax rates, amounts of state and local government securities outstanding, an index of common stock prices, and corporate new capital flotations. The independent variables accounted for 61 percent of the total variation, with most of this coming from the tax rate variable. Her study has several defects, however, which Fitch clearly pointed out.[2] In particular, the weighted (by amounts of taxes paid) average of supramarginal tax rates reflects the differential, since it is used to select the marginal bracket. Thus the correlation which she found may be spurious. Moreover, the weighted average of existing supramarginal tax rates takes no account of anticipated tax rate changes. Finally, the amount of taxes paid is not a good weighting device—individuals heavily invested in tax-exempt securities pay little tax. The weighted average would not correctly reflect their position in municipal bonds.

Identifying the precise effect of variables which have influenced the differential in the past is quite difficult. It is not crucial to do so here, although this would be interesting for future research on the determination of security prices. However, the trend of the relative differential in the postwar period is known. Chart 1 shows the ratio of yields on Aaa and Baa municipals and corporate bonds outstanding, according to Moody's series. As noted in detail below, these yields do not picture "the" differential, but they do give an indication of the trend of the differential, whatever its absolute size.

From the chart it appears that the relative differential (the absolute differential as a percent of corporate yields) diminished through 1954. Since that time it has shown a slight tendency to increase. Aside from this, the spread between yields on the highest and lowest grades of securities have tended toward equality. The differential on Baa-rated securities was much less than that on Aaa-

[1] Lucille Derrick, "Exemption of Security Interest from Income Taxes in the United States," *Journal of Business*, Vol. 19 (October 1946), Pt. 2, pp. 38-49.

[2] Lyle C. Fitch, *Taxing Municipal Bond Income* (University of California Press, 1950), pp. 9-11.

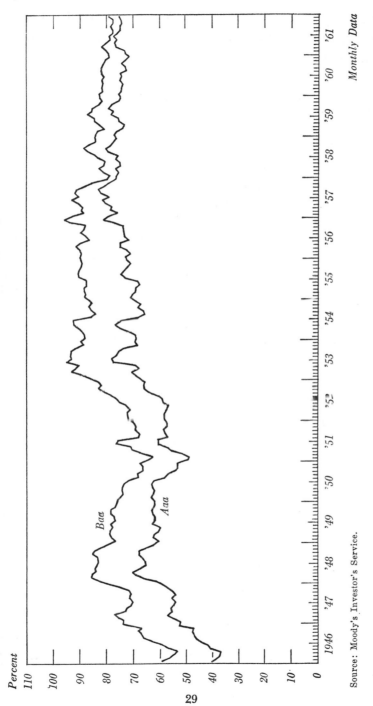

CHART 1. Yields on Outstanding Municipal Bonds as a Percent of Comparable Corporate Bond Yields, 1946-1961

Percent

Source: Moody's Investor's Service.

29

rated securities early in the period; recently the two have come very close together.

What is "the" Yield Differential?

Quantitative Evidence

There are several bits and pieces of quantitative evidence bearing on the level of yields on state and local government securities without the exemption. These include comparisons between yields of corporate and municipal securities between 1900 and 1913, when there was no federal income tax; data for municipal and provincial bonds in Canada, where there is no income tax exemption for interest on local government securities; the experience with railroad equipment trust securities, which, like state-locals are issued in serial form; and yields of bonds issued by religious institutions, which are somewhat similar in character to the securities issued by many of the smaller municipalities in the United States.

CHART 2. Average Annual Yields on Outstanding High-Grade Corporate Bonds and Municipals, 1900-1913

Yield (Percent)

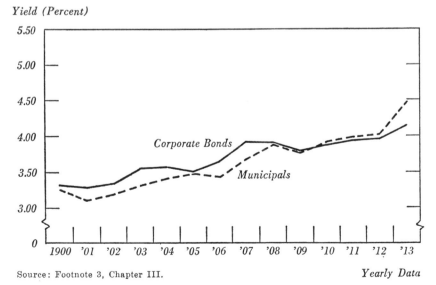

Source: Footnote 3, Chapter III.   *Yearly Data*

CORPORATE AND MUNICIPAL YIELDS, 1900-1913. Chart 2 shows the pattern of average annual yields on "high grade" corporates and municipals between 1900 and 1913. During these fourteen years, municipal yields were about the same as corporate yields. Usually municipals yielded a trifle less, occasionally a trifle more.[3]

The fact that yields on municipals outstanding were usually about the same as yields on corporate bonds outstanding in a period when the tax treatment of interest income on the two was the same gives some support to the hypothesis that restoring equal tax treatment would at least not cause municipal yields generally to rise above corporate yields, whatever the relevant measures are in each case.

THE CANADIAN EXPERIENCE. Canada's experience is also pertinent. Interest on Canadian municipal and provincial bonds is subject to the Canadian income tax. A comparison of these yields with Canadian corporate bond yields should give some indication of what would happen in this country if the exemption feature is dropped.

Chart 3 pictures monthly average yields on outstanding Canadian corporates, provincials, and municipals for 1953 through the first half of 1961.[4] The comparison indicates that the yields on provincials and municipals without the exemption feature are close to average yields on corporates. To the extent that this is relevant to

[3] The measurement of bond yields early in the century is fraught with problems. In those days, the best industrial and utility corporate bonds were not legal for investment by fiduciaries and were not considered by the market to be comparable in quality to the best municipals, which had enjoyed an active investment market for over a hundred years. Thus, a comparison of Standard Statistics Company yields on corporates and municipals shows that for 1900-20 municipals consistently yielded less than corporates, because the Standard Statistics Corporate series contained industrial and utility yields. The yield series used here for corporates is Durand's basic yields for February of each year, with figures for other months interpolated on the basis of Macauley's adjusted railroad bond average. These figures have been averaged to obtain a monthly mean for each year. For municipals, the Bond Buyer's series for "High Grade Municipals" is used. See David Durand, *Basic Yields of Corporate Bonds*, National Bureau of Economic Research, Technical Paper No. 3 (1942), p. 5 and Frederick W. Macauley, *The Movement of Interest Rates, Bond Yields, and Stock Prices in the United States Since 1856* (National Bureau of Economic Research, 1938).

[4] The data are a McCleod, Young, and Weir Company series. No ratings on the industrials or municipals were obtainable. The provincial bonds are all Baa-rated by Moody's.

CHART 3. Yields on Outstanding Canadian Provincial, Municipal, and Industrial Bonds, 1953-1961

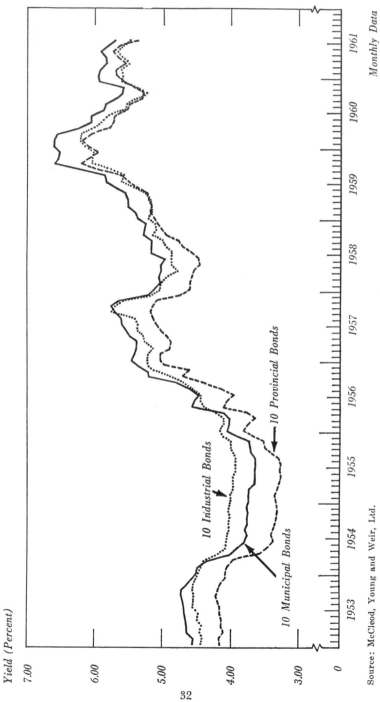

Yield (Percent)

7.00

6.00

5.00

4.00

3.00

0

10 Industrial Bonds

10 Municipal Bonds

10 Provincial Bonds

1953   1954   1955   1956   1957   1958   1959   1960   1961

Monthly Data

Source: McCleod, Young and Weir, Ltd.

the United States case, it suggests again that a comparison of yields on corporates and state and local government bonds of comparable quality roughly would indicate "the true" differential. Not too much weight should be put on this evidence, however. First, the series used are averages, and the "mix" of bonds of various qualities in the three series will affect relative yields. There is no evidence on the quality ratings of bonds included in the industrial or municipal series. Second, the large flows of United States capital to Canada may have affected relative yields in recent years, for example, by depressing the corporate yield relative to others. Finally, as discussed previously, there may be a significant divergence in the behavior of yields on outstandings and on new issues. Some limited evidence suggests that this is the case in Canada.[5]

It has also been suggested that a comparison of new issue yields on Canadian municipals and provincials floated in American markets may be indicative of the "true" differential.[6] These bonds are taxable and are rated by the same investment advisory services which rate United States tax-exempts, so a comparison can be made grade by grade. For 1959, the data shown in Table 2 have been compiled.

The spread between yields on new issues of taxable Canadian municipals and provincials and the IBA median new issue yield for like quality United States municipal issues was in every case greater than that between United States new issue (public) corporate bonds and the IBA yields. In some cases, the difference is substantial. For what these data are worth, they suggest that taxable Canadian issues have higher yields than comparable quality American corporate issues. The significance of this evidence is doubtful, how-

[5] A check of new issue yields in 1960 and 1961 on Canadian corporates and provincials, as reported in *The Financial Post* (Toronto), shows that provincials were issued at lower yields, on the average, than corporate new issues. In 1960, the average yield on 23 provincials was 5.77 percent while on 41 corporates it was 6.42 percent. The 1961 figures were 5.64 percent for 30 provincials and 6.17 percent for 48 corporates. The yields were on issues of some $484 million of provincials and $712 million of corporates in 1960, and $700 million and $362 million respectively in 1961. Unfortunately, the same comparison could not be made for each credit category—no ratings were available.

[6] See statement of Harvey Brazer and discussion by Cushman McGee, House Committee on Ways and Means, *Income Tax Revision*, Panel Discussions, 86 Cong. 1 sess. (1960), pp. 168, 394-96.

ever. Although these bonds are denominated in United States dollars, there is still the risk of money exchange problems which may result in an increase in the differential.

RAILROAD EQUIPMENT TRUST OBLIGATIONS. A gauge of yields on the higher grade state and local government securities without the exemption feature might be a series of new issue yields on railroad equipment trust obligations. These are practically the only corporate securities issued in serial form. Since some analysts attach importance to serial form as a factor affecting marketability and the yield differential, it is interesting to compare the new issue yields on comparably rated equipment obligations and corporate bonds.

TABLE 2. Comparison of Reoffering Yields of Canadian and United States Municipal Securities Sold in the United States

Rating	Date of Issue	Canadian Securities	United States Securities	Canadian-United States Differential	United States Municipal-Corporate Differential
		(1)	(2)	(3)	(4)
Aa	4/21/59	4.89%	3.33%	1.56%	1.15%
A	1/14/59	4.85	3.60	1.25	1.04
A	6/24/59	5.13	3.90	1.23	1.01
A	7/ 2/59	5.38	3.95	1.43	1.01
A	7/16/59	5.00	3.95	1.05	1.01
A	8/20/59	5.00	3.15	1.85	1.22
A	10/21/59	5.63	3.80	1.83	1.47

Sources:
   Column (1), House Committee on Ways and Means, *Income Tax Revision*, 86 Cong. 1 sess., p. 395.
   Column (2), Median yield of Investment Bankers' Association series, from Appendix Table 3.
   Column (3), Col. 1 less Col. 2.
   Column (4), Based on FHA corporate yields from Appendix Table 2 and municipal yields from Appendix Table 3.

The data in Table 3 suggest that little significance can be attached to the allegation that the serial form of issue significantly affects yields on a security. The data show that with few exceptions serials sold at yields lower than the average for all corporate issues. Not too much weight should be attached to the size of the spreads, however, for there are intricate problems in comparing serials and term issues. The fact that yields on railroad bonds are being compared with yields on all corporate bonds affects the computed differences. Moreover, there is little assurance that the quality ratings are

TABLE 3. Reoffering Yields on Railroad Equipment Obligations and Corporates, 1959

Issue and Quality		Reoffering Yield (15 years)	Comparable Corporate (Avg. for mo.)	Col. (1) Minus Col. (2)
		(1)	(2)	(3)
AAA				
2/4	Denver and Rio Grande Sec. X	4.25%	4.42%	—0.17%
4/2	Norfolk and Western	4.30	4.40	—0.10
5/14	Chesapeake & Ohio	4.55	4.60	—0.05
5/26	Norfolk and Western	4.65	4.60	0.05
8/13	Chesapeake & Ohio	4.60	4.85	—0.25
AA				
1/4	Louisville & Nashville	4.25	4.48	—0.23
1/20	Chicago, Burlington & Quincy	4.40	4.48	—0.08
2/10	Northern Pacific Railway	4.35	4.48	—0.13
2/24	Chicago, Rock Island & Pacific	4.20	4.48	—0.28
3/12	Illinois Central	4.25	4.41	—0.16
3/26	Texas and Pacific	4.20[a]	4.41	—0.21
4/7	Pittsburgh & Lake Erie	4.40	4.48	—0.08
5/6	Great Northern Railway	4.55	4.64	—0.09
6/4	Seaboard Airlines	4.70	4.77	—0.07
6/18	Chicago, Burlington & Quincy	4.70	4.69	0.01
7/7	Northern Pacific Railway	4.75	4.69	0.06
8/11	Illinois Central	4.65	4.76	—0.11
8/24	Seaboard Airlines	4.65	4.76	—0.11
8/26	Pittsburgh & Lake Erie	4.70	4.76	—0.06
9/9	Chicago, Burlington & Quincy	4.90	5.04	—0.14
12/16	Northern Pacific	4.85	5.16	—0.31
A				
1/21	Chicago, Milwaukee, St. Paul & Pacific	4.65	4.62	0.03
2/18	Southern Pacific Co.	4.40	4.47	—0.07
4/1	Southern Pacific Co.	4.45	4.64	—0.19
6/24	Southern Pacific Co.	4.80	4.91	—0.11
7/16	Missouri Pacific	4.85	4.96	—0.11
8/27	Southern Pacific Co.	4.85	5.02	—0.17
9/2	Wabash R.R.	5.00	5.22	—0.22
9/30	Missouri Pacific	5.20	5.22	—0.02
11/4	Southern Pacific	4.95	5.37	—0.42
Baa				
1/6	Chicago & Northwestern R.R.	5.13	4.98	0.15

Sources:
Column (1): Data furnished by Salomon Bros. & Hutzler.
Column (2): FHA new issue yield series, from App. Table 2.
[a] 10 years.

precise enough to justify such close comparison. However, the evidence does not suggest that serials would have substantially higher yields than the general yield averages.

ISSUES BY RELIGIOUS INSTITUTIONS. The discussion in Chapter II indicates that one of the questions frequently raised in connection with any attempt to remove the exemption feature is: What will happen to the small, unrated issues? The basic problem here is one of determining the yields at which these issues would sell without the exemption. Obviously, they can be placed at some yield, however high. Implicit in the emphasis given by those favoring retention is that the yields demanded by investors will be "too" high for these borrowers to pay without assistance.

Note here that we are concerned only with small unrated issues. The large unrated issues evidently would not suffer in this respect, as will be indicated shortly. But the current selling practice is to offer such small issues in local markets to buyers who particularly benefit from the exemption feature. It is maintained that these small borrowers would face substantial yield premiums should the interest income become fully taxable.

An indication of what yields on these small issues might be if interest on them were fully taxable is the yield on small, unrated religious bonds. These include bonds issued by church groups for building purposes, both at churches themselves and for church-related hospitals, schools, etc. Open markets in these securities are virtually nonexistent, and investment in them is somewhat local, as in the case of small issues of municipals.[7] Many investors, including institutions, are not aware of them, as the investment bankers handling them testify. Further, holders of bonds issued by religious institutions come from somewhat the same investor groups as those holding small-sized municipals—individuals (50 percent), banks, and insurance companies. They are attracted for much the same reasons, for example, yield, depositor relationships, and local pride.[8]

[7] A representative of a large dealer in these issues (B.C. Ziegler & Co.) estimates that at present annual issues of religious bonds are about $150 million.

[8] We are informed of one interesting explanation for the fact that fraternal life societies buy religious bond issues so extensively. Apparently, the sale of their life insurance policies is at least not injured by having ministers who will recommend

TABLE 4. Reoffering Yields on Selected Small Issues of Fully
Taxable Religious Bonds, 1959–60

Issuer and Date	Size of Issue	Reoffering Yields			
		1 Year	5 Years	10 Years	15 Years
		1959			
Memorial Hospital, Neillsville, Wisconsin, 2/18/59	$175,000	5.00%	5.00%	5.25%	5.75[a]%
Congregation of Immanuel Evangelical Church, Danville, Illinois, 1/19/59	235,000	4.75	5.00	5.25	5.50
Wauwatosa Presbyterian Church, 1/28/59	250,000	5.00	5.25	5.50	5.50
St. Joseph Memorial Hospital of Kokomo, 3/19/59	200,000	4.75	5.00	5.13	5.13[a]
Immanuel Baptist Church of Tulsa, 3/26/59	275,000	5.00	5.25	5.50	—
		1960			
St. Bernard's Congregation, 5/16/60	200,000	5.00	5.00	5.50	5.50
St. Maria Goretti Congregation, 9/23/60	230,000	5.00	—	5.50	5.75
St. Thomas Aquinas, 2/1/60	225,000	—	5.50	5.75	5.75
Lakeland College, 10/12/60	275,000	5.00	5.25	5.75	5.75
Cargill Methodist Church, Janesville, Wisconsin, 2/1/60	260,000	—	5.75	6.00	6.00
First Baptist Church of Pasadena, California, 6/3/60	200,000	—	5.75	—	—

Source: B. C. Ziegler & Co.
[a] 14 years

In Table 4, a small but fairly representative sample of small-sized bond issues is shown for 1959-60. None of these issues exceeded $275,000. They were sold at the yields indicated. These data suggest a range of long-term yields on small unrated religious bonds of about 5.5 to 6 percent. By contrast, the FHA new issue yields on public offerings of corporate bonds ranged, in 1959-60, from a low of 4.7 percent to a high of 5.71 percent.[9] If religious bond yields are a reliable gauge, yields between 5.5 and 6 percent would be a rea-

---

them to inquiring members desiring insurance, and the minister would certainly tend to recall the name of the company holding the church mortgage bonds.

[9] Mortimer Kaplan, "Yields on Recently Issued Corporate Bonds: A New Index," *Journal of Finance*, Vol. 17 (March 1962), Appendix.

sonable approximation of yields on small unrated municipals issued without the exemption feature if the level of rates prevailing in 1959-60 is maintained. We shall come back to this problem shortly.

Judgments of Capital Market Experts

The question of what after removal yields on municipal obligations would be is intimately bound up with the operations and reactions of the capital markets. The fact that any alternative yield series will have to be based on qualitative evidence and judgment suggested that one useful way of pursuing the problem was to survey those who make such judgments daily. The following paragraphs give a general summary of views expressed in interviews with leading capital market participants on the questions of yields on municipals without the exemption feature and the general reaction of the market to removal of exemption. These individuals were not chosen as specialists in municipal bonds or as spokesmen for particular views on the exemption feature. Rather, they were chosen as individuals with intimate knowledge of the portfolio decisions of investment managers of large financial institutions.

Out of these discussions there emerged an interesting consensus on the reaction of yields in the capital markets to exemption removal. In brief, these experts felt that removal of the exemption feature would cause a general rise in yields on all fixed-interest-bearing securities. They suggested that individuals would shift out of tax-exempts and into non-fixed-interest-bearing assets, such as equities and real estate. As yields on municipals rose, some investors, particularly life insurance companies and corporate pension funds, would enter the market for municipals more aggressively, diverting some of the cash inflow previously designated for corporate bonds and mortgages. As a group, they felt that life insurance companies and pension funds would hold a greater proportion of their fixed-interest-bearing securities in the form of municipals. Individuals, in their judgment, would divert some of their holdings of municipal bonds to other assets. On balance, the supply of funds to the fixed-interest-bearing segment of the capital market would be reduced, and, given the volume of flotations, average yields on such securities would tend to rise. In the final analysis, yields on state and local government securities would approximate those of corporates, grade for grade, but corporate yields would be somewhat higher than they are now.

This is the general picture traced, with variations, by every capital market participant interviewed. Several other points were also commonly made in elaboration. First, by "the" yield on corporate bonds, which presumably would rise, capital market experts do not mean Moody's yields on outstandings or even Moody's new issue yields. It was pointed out time and again that these series are not indicative of "the" yield on corporate bonds in the sense used above. The yield series should be a new issue series, but it should account for the new issue yields on the much more important private placements in addition to the present yield series on public offerings. In recent years, private placements of corporate bond issues have been some 50 percent of total issues. At these yields state and local government securities would attract investment managers of life insurance companies and pension funds. Alternatively, mortgage yields might reflect yield levels that state and local governments would have to pay to compete in the fixed interest-bearing portion of the capital market.

Second, the experts interviewed felt that the term structure of yields on municipals would be much more like the corporate pattern, that is, the yield curve would have much less upward slope. Weakening of support by banks, primarily interested in short-dated obligations, and the more plentiful supply of funds offered at the long end by life insurance companies and pension funds were suggested as the principal factors leading to a flatter yield curve.

Third, the experts felt that the structure of yields by credit rating without the exemption feature might be flatter—the lower-rated municipalities might sell at yields much closer to high grade yields than they do with the exemption feature. They reasoned that life insurance companies have been very aggressive buyers of the low rated high-yielding taxable securities, much more so than banks and personal trust departments. Several developments explain this concentration by life insurance companies on low-rated high-yielding investments. (1) Research studies (which they helped to finance)[10] have shown that higher returns on low-grade bonds have historically been more than enough to offset higher default losses. (2)The younger investment managers who have come into positions of authority since World War II accept the thesis that government will prevent any general economic collapse, that the risk of default on all obligations is reduced. (3) Life insurance companies have had to earn high yields to compete in the pension business with un-insured pension funds which concentrate on equities. The weakening of interest by the banks and personal trust departments would raise Aaa and Aa yields in relation to yields on lower quality issues, since they are particularly active in these rating classes. The aggressive activity of life insurance companies and corporate pension funds would lower relative yields in the lower credit rating classes.

Interesting observations were also made with regard to the effects of removing the exemption on yields of small issues. The specialists generally agreed that if small issues did not appeal to the large life insurance companies and corporate pension funds, they might experience a relative rise in reoffering yields. It was noted, however, that life insurance companies had purchased considerable amounts of small issues of revenue bonds in the immediate postwar period. Moreover, the experts confirmed the judgment expressed above that the smaller local insurance companies could be expected to express considerable interest in state and local securities at the higher yields which would prevail. And they felt that tax benefits written into state tax laws would provide an additional stimulus.

Some of those interviewed firmly rejected the view that any special problem of "smallness" would attach to municipals because of the serial form of issue. If yields on municipals were attractive relative to corporates, they maintained, no discount would attach to them because they are serially issued. Buyers take the "strips" of maturities they desire at time of offering. Since life insurance companies and corporate pension funds ordinarily do not sell in the secondary market,[11] their portfolio managers choose bond invest-

---

[10] In particular, W. Braddock Hickman's *Corporate Bonds: Quality and Investment Performance*, National Bureau of Economic Research, Occasional Paper No. 59 (1957), p. 16.

[11] This was verified in an unpublished study done by the Life Insurance Association of America for the Securities and Exchange Commission. In this study it was

ments which they plan to hold to maturity. Thus, municipalities would not be penalized if they continued to use the serial form.

An Alternative Series

The discussions with capital market experts lead us to conclude that "the" relevant yield on taxable securities can be viewed conceptually as some sort of weighted average of new issue yields on public offerings and private placements of corporate bonds. In other words, the relevant comparable rate on taxable securities, grade by grade and maturity by maturity, is somewhere between the yields on publicly and privately placed issues.

Data are available on both private placement and new issue corporate bond yields. The private placement yield series is a compilation by the Life Insurance Association of America and shows yields at time of commitment. There are a number of problems in using this series because of the method of credit rating used, differences in monthly sample size, possible errors in reporting, etc. In collecting these data from insurance companies, the association requests that each placement have a rating attached comparable to those supplied by Moody's Investor's Service for public issues. The rating is done by the insurance company, however, so we cannot be certain that the standards applied are identical. A second problem is that no term structure is available for yields on private placements. Only a single, and obviously long-term, average yield was computed. Third, the number of commitments in the higher credit ratings is (reflecting the low-rating, high-yield policies mentioned earlier) very small and in some months zero. Thus there are gaps in the yield series in these categories. Lastly, the data are available only for the period since September 1959, and not continuously in the form most appropriate to the present problem. Nevertheless, the annual averages are probably reasonably accurate measures of the level of private placement yields for the lower quality bonds.

The placement yield data most pertinent to our problem are summarized in Table 5, where the average yields on rated and unrated private placements and the average monthly yield are pre-

---

estimated that 16 companies with 73 percent of the assets of life insurance companies had resales of 1.22 percent of their private placements.

TABLE 5. Average Yields on Commitments of Private Placements of Corporate Bonds by Life Insurance Companies, Monthly, 1960

Month	1st Quality	2nd Quality	3rd Quality	4th Quality	Unclassified[b]	Total
January	—[a]	5.83%	5.89%	6.15%	6.08%	6.04%
February	—[a]	5.57	5.69	6.15	6.17	6.04
March	5.94	5.72	5.66	6.07	6.32	5.94
April	—[a]	—[a]	5.77	6.01	6.30	6.05
May	—[a]	—[a]	5.82	6.01	6.89	6.00
June	—[a]	5.55	5.89	6.08	6.43	6.07
July	—[a]	5.85	5.68	6.09	5.95	5.91
August	—[a]	—[a]	5.79	5.85	6.12	5.88
September	—[a]	—[a]	5.69	5.86	6.07	5.84
October	—[a]	—[a]	5.79	5.67	6.32	5.93
November	—[a]	4.99	5.45	5.85	5.77	5.65
December	—[c]	—[c]	—[c]	—[c]	6.05	5.96

Source: Life Insurance Association of America.
[a] Not more than one commitment—thus no compilation.
[b] These data include single authorizations.
[c] No data available.

sented for 1960. It will be noted that in only one month were there enough commitments of "1st Quality" bonds to justify a yield computation for this category. An average for "2nd Quality" bonds could be computed in only six out of eleven months.

There are also data available on new issue yields of public issues of corporate bonds. We have chosen to use the FHA series, which is based on monthly averages of Friday yields of recently issued Aaa to Baa bonds (Moody-rated). These are computed from quotations listed in the weekly statistical edition of *The Commercial and Financial Chronicle*.[12] The 1960 FHA data on new public issue yields are presented in Table 6; and, in Chart 4, A- and Baa-rated public issue yields are compared to "3rd Quality" and "4th Quality" private placement yields.

In view of the lack of observations in the higher credit categories of private corporate placements, no weighted average of the FHA and private placement series can be computed for each credit category. Even if it could be computed, the result would not be al-

[12] The complete series is given for 1951-61 in Appendix Table 2.

TABLE 6. Monthly Average Yields of Recently Issued Corporate Bonds, 1960

Month	Aaa	Aa	A	Baa
January	5.11%	5.09%	5.04%	5.31%
February	5.01	4.96	5.03	5.71
March	4.96	4.93	4.87	5.64
April	4.93	4.85	4.95	5.51
May	4.89	4.90	5.09	5.30
June	4.80	4.85	5.06	5.40
July	4.71	4.73	4.93	5.38
August	4.55	4.60	4.70	5.15
September	4.62	4.61	4.68	5.10
October	4.65	4.64	4.77	5.11
November	4.69	4.67	4.91	—ᵃ
December	4.72	4.78	4.78	—ᵃ

Source: App. Table 2.
ᵃ No data available.

CHART 4. Yields on Comparable Grades of Public and Private Placements of Corporate Bonds, 1960

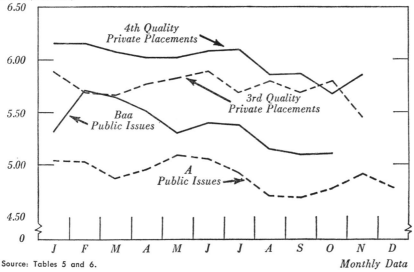

Yield (Percent)

4th Quality Private Placements

3rd Quality Private Placements

Baa Public Issues

A Public Issues

Source: Tables 5 and 6.   Monthly Data

43

together satisfactory. One reason is that there are problems in using the weighted average to measure the alternative yield or in using the differential between this average and exempt municipal yields as a gauge of the rise in interest costs. The assumption would be that the yield structure of municipals by credit category without exemption would parallel that for corporates. Another reason is that there is no assurance that "the" yield on municipals by quality class would rise exactly to the weighted average of private placement and public issue yields. In the general change in all yield levels it might fall on either side.

The two series can be used, however, to get a general range for yields on municipals without exemption and the differential between these and current (with exemption) yields (Chart 4). This range is estimated for long-term yields in Table 7. There the "3rd Quality" yields on private placements and the approximately comparable "A" public corporate issue yields are compared with the IBA median yields on "A" 20-year general obligation municipals.

TABLE 7. Differentials Between Long-Term Yields on 3rd Quality Private Placements and A-Rated Public Corporate Bonds and Municipals, 1960

Month	Private Placement Yields	Public Corporate Bond Yields	20-Year Municipal Yields	Differential (1) − (3)	Differential (2) − (3)
	(1)	(2)	(3)	(4)	(5)
January	5.89%	5.04%	4.10%	1.79%	0.94%
February	5.69	5.03	3.85	1.84	1.18
March	5.66	4.87	3.73	1.93	1.14
April	5.77	4.95	3.75	2.02	1.20
May	5.82	5.09	3.78	2.04	1.31
June	5.89	5.06	3.60	2.29	1.46
July	5.68	4.93	3.75	1.93	1.18
August	5.79	4.70	3.50	2.29	1.20
September	5.69	4.68	3.60	2.09	1.08
October	5.79	4.77	3.70	2.09	1.07
November	5.45	4.91	3.55	1.90	1.36
December	—a	4.78	3.60	—	1.18
Average	—	—	—	2.02	1.19

Sources: Column (1): Table 5;   Column (2): Table 6;   Column (3): App. Table 3.
a No data available.

TABLE 8. Estimated Range of New Issue Reoffering Yields of Long-Term Municipals Without Exemption, 1960[a]

Month	Aaa		Aa		A		Baa		Unrated[b]	
	Low	High	Low	High	Low	High	Low	High	Low	High
January	4.57%	5.41%	4.84%	5.68%	5.29%	6.10%	5.49%	6.33%	5.39%	6.22%
February	4.69	5.43	4.64	5.48	5.04	5.88	5.44	6.28	5.74	6.08
March	4.49	5.33	4.64	5.48	4.92	5.76	5.37	6.21	5.14	5.99
April	4.39	5.23	4.62	5.46	4.94	5.78	5.29	6.13	5.12	5.96
May	4.49	5.33	4.59	5.43	4.97	5.81	5.29	6.13	5.13	5.97
June	4.39	5.21	4.54	5.38	4.79	5.63	5.24	6.08	5.02	5.86
July	4.34	5.18	4.59	5.43	4.94	5.78	5.19	6.03	5.07	5.91
August	4.14	4.98	4.34	5.18	4.69	5.53	4.99	5.83	4.83	5.68
September	4.29	5.13	4.49	5.33	4.79	5.63	5.02	5.86	4.91	5.73
October	4.32	5.26	4.54	5.38	4.89	5.73	5.14	5.98	5.02	5.86
November	4.19	5.03	4.39	5.23	4.74	5.58	5.04	5.88	5.89	5.73
December	4.27	5.11	4.44	5.28	4.79	5.63	5.07	5.91	5.93	5.77

[a] Lows and highs for rated issues obtained by adding to IBA 20-year median yields 119 and 202 basis points, respectively.
[b] Average of lows and highs of A and Baa yields.

For 1960, the differential between private placements and municipals ranged from 179 basis points to 229 basis points. Leaving out the lower extreme the range is from 184 to 229. For the eleven months, the average differential was 202 basis points. The differential between "A-rated" corporate public issue yields and the "A-rated" IBA 20-year municipal yields ranged from 94 to 146 basis points and averaged 119 basis points.

On the basis of this evidence, we assume that the average alternative long-term yield (without exemption) on rated municipals for 1960 was 119-202 basis points more than the IBA 20-year municipal yield for each rating class. The range of yields obtained is shown for each category for 1960 in Table 8.

The unrated issues pose special problems. As Frank E. Morris has shown,[13] the unrated issues are not always lower in quality than the Baa issues. For the month he studied, median yields on unrated issues were below median yields on Baa issues. This suggests that the market considered their quality to be higher on the average. As mentioned previously, issues are unrated when the outstanding in-

[13] Frank E. Morris, "The Structure of Interest Rates on Municipal Bonds," *IBA Statistical Bulletin* (July 1958), pp. 1-4.

debtedness of the issuing authority is small or zero. Revenue issues, even though large, may be unrated if there is insufficient operating experience. The range of yields on unrated issues is extremely broad, that is, they vary widely in quality.

In the same article, Morris showed that no yield premium was required for small issues because of their size. If the average yield on these unrated issues falls between A and Baa yields, without the exemption, small issues will face no additional special problems. The concentration of these issues in the unrated category would not raise the median yields for that category above Baa yields.[14] In short, if Morris' results are extrapolated, smallness per se would neither require a yield premium nor raise relative yields on all unrated issues.

Two additional pieces of evidence bear on this judgment. First, there is the information presented earlier on religious issues. The second is the size distribution of yields on private placements. Longer-term yields on new issues of small religious bonds ranged from about 5.5 percent to 6 percent. When this range is compared with the alternative yield series in Table 8 it fits between the A and Baa yields without exemption, about where Morris' study indicated for all unrated issues. This suggests again that small size per se would not reflect differentially on yields in the unrated group.

A size distribution of yields on private placements would indicate whether the large institutional buyers, who might dominate the market after the exemption is removed, require yield premiums which vary inversely with the size of issue. No data are available on this, and the Life Insurance Association's basic data do not permit a compilation. However, those familiar with these placements indicated that there is considerable variation in yields by size of loan. Smaller loans are placed at substantially higher yields now. On the other hand, this information is prepared from data submitted by some twenty-five to forty of the largest life insurance companies, whose transaction costs for small placements may be higher per dollar of yield than those of the smaller companies. The yield premiums which they describe may be overstated.

In short, the evidence on this point is not wholly conclusive.

---

[14] For 1957-58, issues of under $1 million accounted for 8,015 out of 8,494 issues in the unrated category, and for about half the dollar volume. *IBA Statistical Bulletin* (August 1959), pp. 2-3.

The evidence available from the religious bond yields suggests, however, that the average long-term yields on unrated issues will fall somewhere between the A and Baa yields. This implies little change from the results which Morris found. In light of this, the low and high unrated yields (without exemption) are assumed to be the average of low and high Baa and A yields given in Table 8. These are the low and high figures entered in the "unrated" column in that table.

Thus our tentative conclusion is that in 1960 long-term yields on state and local government bonds would have risen by 119-202 basis points if there had been no tax exemption for the income from such bonds. These results are subject to some qualifications. First, bond yields move with the cycle. The spread between the FHA series on recently issued corporates and the IBA median yield series on new issues of tax-exempts is greater in 1960 than for the average 1957-60. This difference, 15 basis points for both Baa and Aa rated bonds, is an element of overstatement of the rise in yields of new municipal issues in our calculation. Second, deviations of yields from the median IBA yield appear to be skewed. Examination of the mean and median IBA yields on Aa-rated 20-year bonds shows that the median yield was less than the mean yield in 48 of the 60 months, July 1956-June 1961. On the average, the median was 3 basis points lower than the mean. This difference will also be subtracted from the tentative estimates.

Allowing for these qualifications suggests that long-term yields on municipals would rise within the limits of 101-184 basis points.

To obtain an estimate of the full rise in interest costs if the exemption feature is removed, the change of yields in the shorter maturities should also be known. This requires an estimate of the change in the slope of the yield curve for municipals with exemption removal. The yield curve of municipals with the exemption feature is clearly "steeper" than the yield curve for corporates, though obtaining the latter is somewhat difficult.[15] This suggests that removal of the exemption feature will cause yields on the shorter maturities of municipals to rise more than long-term yields. Indeed, it will be recalled from the discussions with capital market experts, summarized above, that their general opinion was

[15] See the discussion by Roland I. Robinson, *The Postwar Market of State and Local Government Securities* (National Bureau of Economic Research, 1960), pp. 180-88.

that the term structure of yields on municipals without the exemption would be much "flatter" than the present curve. There was a consensus that it would closely resemble the term structure on corporate bonds.

Whether in fact the yield curve for municipals would flatten out and resemble the corporate yield curve if the exemption feature is removed depends on the factors causing the differences in the slopes of the two curves now. More basically it depends on the forces determining the shape of yield curves generally. The capital market experts based their prediction of a lessening of the municipal yield curve slope on what might be called an institutional approach to yield-maturity relationships—a lessening of support by banks, who buy short- and intermediate-term maturities, and an increase in the support by life insurance companies, who are mainly buyers of long maturity serials.

What factors have influenced the observed shape of the yield curve for municipal bonds? Three principal effects seem to be at work. First, the practice of selling high-coupon short serials and and deep-discount long serials makes the curve steeper than a comparable curve for corporates. This is so because of capital gains taxation. Deep discount bonds sell at a higher yield because the capital gains tax must be paid on the difference between purchase and redemption prices. Conversely, high coupon, premium serials sell at lower yields because they afford capital losses which can be taken at time of sale or maturity. In particular, banks have been able to charge capital losses against current income at the 52 percent rate.[16]

In the market for corporate bonds, where interest income is taxable, deep discount bonds sell at a premium, other things equal; high coupon bonds sell at a discount. The reason again is not hard to find. Since the tax rate applicable to interest income is more than the capital gains rate, buyers prefer deep discount bonds, that is, prefer to receive income as a capital gain. Thus the practice of selling high coupon and deep discount bonds explains some of the observed slope of the tax-exempt yield curve.

Second, some economic theorists have concluded that upward sloping yield curves reflect expectations of higher yields. If expected further increases in the relative supply of municipals have led to

[16] Presumably this explains some of their interest in higher coupon serials.

the anticipation of higher future yields, this would have contribu-
ted also to the observed slope of the municipal yield curve. To the
extent that elimination of tax-exemption reduces the projected future supply of state and local securities, this too will contribute to a
flattening of the curve in the future.

Third, anticipated future tax rate changes affect the slope of the
municipal yield curve. The more future tax rates are expected to
exceed present tax rates, the lower long-term yields will be relative
to short-term yields and conversely. This conclusion follows from
the analysis presented earlier in this chapter and needs little further
discussion here.

It is difficult to separate these three effects—and possibly others
—to measure the direction of each effect on the present yield curve
for state and local securities. Combining such an analysis with the
earlier discussion of changes in long-term yields is unlikely to produce useful conclusions. In short, this analysis leads to a conclusion
similar to the one stated by market experts on the basis of institutional factors. Both suggest that the after-removal yield curve for
taxed municipals will be flatter than at present. Neither, however,
suggests a method of estimating just how much flattening can be
expected.

Specific charting of yield curves for the alternative yield series
is not very feasible. Thus, in the next chapter when the rise in interest costs to state and local governments is estimated, we shall
assume that yields in all maturities rise by the same number of percentage points. Then we shall roughly gauge the maximum effect
of removing the exemption on the term structure of municipal bond
yields. Some allowance for term structure will be made in the estimate of the interest cost increase.

In summary, in this chapter it has been tentatively suggested
that long-term yields on state and local government bonds in recent
years would likely have risen by some 101-184 basis points had the
exemption feature not been in effect. There would have been a
somewhat greater rise in short-term yields. We shall now see what
effect such an increase would have had on interest payments if the
exemption feature had not been in effect in 1960 and will then estimate what additional federal revenue would have been obtained
from a tax on municipal bond income.

CHAPTER IV

New Estimates of Interest Saving

TO ESTIMATE the change in Treasury revenue from new issues of state and local securities, issued without the exemption feature, provision must be made for changes in ownership, differences in applicable marginal tax rates, and other complicating factors. These problems are analyzed in this and the following chapter before an estimate of the revenue yield of the tax is provided.

First, the analysis of the previous chapter is applied to estimate the effect of removing tax exemption on the interest cost of state and local governments. Then a new estimate of the revenue gain to the federal government is made and the revenue gain is compared to the increase in interest cost. The comparison strongly suggests that removal of tax exemption will yield a net revenue gain to the federal government. In a final section of Chapter V the additional revenues state and local governments would receive from taxing federal interest payments are estimated for comparison.

Previous Estimates

Before attempting to estimate the expected rise in interest costs of state-local governments that removal of the exemption feature

50

would produce, a more detailed look at some problems connected with the techniques employed in previous estimates is instructive.

Measuring the interest cost saving to state and local governments in any year due to the exemption feature poses two principal problems. First, some judgment must be made about what the yield on state and local government securities would be if they were fully taxable. As just seen, this is not a simple task. Second, the interest payments (cost) on such securities in any year consists of payments contracted in all previous periods in which the debt currently outstanding was issued. The contractual payment in each case depended on the market yield of state and local government securities at the time of issue. Assume that the interest income on all municipals was subject to tax at time of issue. The change in current interest payments by state and local governments then depends (1) on the time distribution of presently outstanding issues and (2) the difference in interest cost between taxable and exempt bonds for each year and each maturity class.

Both of these difficulties are serious, so much so that no study has overcome them as yet. Most investigators have instead satisfied themselves with very crude indicators. Yields on state and local government securities with taxation have been commonly estimated by yields of outstanding corporate bonds of the same credit category. The second difficulty has typically been avoided by simply taking as a measure of interest cost saving the product of the value of outstandings times "the" yield differential in basis points. On this assumption, the interest cost savings for 1960 would be:

value of outstandings (average—1960)..........$ 66.7 billion
times yield differential (average—1960, Moody's). ×1.04 percentage points
_____
equals interest cost savings....................$693.7 million

This estimate can be improved by dividing outstandings and yields into credit categories and summing the computation for each, but the same basic problems remain.

Robinson sought to avoid the problem of dating outstandings by developing an estimate of the "first year" interest cost savings on new issues[1] instead of an estimate of the total annual interest cost

[1] Roland I. Robinson, *Postwar Market for State and Local Government Securities* (National Bureau of Economic Research, 1960), pp. 194-95.

saving for any year. Gross sales were broken down by credit category. The "first year" interest saving was computed for each rating class by multiplying the difference between the yield on tax-exempts outstanding and corporates outstanding with the same (Moody's) credit rating times gross sales for that rating group.[2] However, this procedure is based on certain additional assumptions. In particular, the basis-point differential times new issues would approximate the "first year" interest cost savings only in special circumstances. If state and local government securities were term bonds, the initial interest payment would be higher by the basis-point differential times new issues. Robinson's estimate would be essentially correct. For example, a term bond paying $3.00 per annum would sell at $100 if new issue yields were 3 percent; if new issue yields were 4 percent, the same $100 would cost $4.00 per annum. Initial interest costs would be higher by the 1 percentage point difference times the volume of new issues.

But if the issue were in serial form with different coupons, the change in the "first year" interest cost would reflect the changed term structure of yields and the maturity pattern of the issue. Suppose that instead of a term bond the issue of bonds by a state or local authority with the exemption feature in effect is as shown in Table 9. The "first year" interest cost of $513,700 reflects coupons set on all the fifteen serials. Now suppose a higher yield series reflecting the absence of the exemption feature is substituted. Specifically, assume that all the yields shown in the table are higher by 100 basis points (1 percent). Each coupon will now have to be raised by approximately 1 percentage point to get the same total revenue from each serial. In this case, the additional "first year" interest cost would be higher by the basis points change times the total issue, that is, $0.01 \times \$15,000,000 = \$150,000$.

Robinson used a basis-point differential derived at the long end of the term structure. As long as yields for all terms rise by the same number of basis points, his assumption is valid that the increment in "first year" interest cost equals the differential times the gross

---

[2] To make the total figure for interest cost savings comparable to the revenue lost estimate based on net issues, he then divided this figure by a ratio of net purchases by taxable investors to gross issues of new securities.

TABLE 9. A Hypothetical State or Local Bond 15-Year Issue

Maturing in (Years)	Amount (par)	Coupon Rate	Offering Yield	Production[a]	Annual Interest Payments	Interest Cost per Year
1	$1,300,000	5.00%	1.75%	100.24	$65,000	$513,700
2	300,000	5.00	2.00	105.85	15,000	448,700
3	300,000	5.00	2.20	108.09	15,000	433,700
4	300,000	5.00	2.35	110.06	15,000	418,700
5	300,000	5.00	2.50	111.68	15,000	403,700
6	1,300,000	5.00	2.65	112.96	15,000	388,700
7	1,300,000	5.00	2.80	113.90	65,000	373,700
8	1,300,000	3.00	2.90	100.71	39,000	308,700
9	1,300,000	3.00	3.00	100.00	39,000	269,700
10	1,300,000	3.00	3.05	99.57	39,000	230,700
11	1,300,000	3.10	3.10	100.00	40,300	191,700
12	1,300,000	3.10	3.15	99.45	40,300	151,400
13	1,300,000	3.20	3.20	100.00	41,600	111,100
14	1,100,000	3.25	3.30	99.44	35,750	69,500
15	1,000,000	3.375	3.40	99.71	33,750	33,750

[a] Production is the total revenue to the syndicate (given by coupon for each serial and market yield for that serial) stated as a percentage of par.

issue. However, there is no special assurance that the term structure of yields without the exemption would rise by the same basis-point amount at every maturity. When it does not, his assumption—though perhaps proximate—is not strictly accurate. For example, should the shorter maturities rise by more than 1 basis point in the example, the "first year" interest cost would be greater than that indicated by the Robinson assumption; the reverse would hold if the shorter maturities rose by less than 1 basis point.

Finally, Robinson uses yields on different grades of outstanding corporate bonds as a standard of what the yields on tax-exempts would be if they were taxable. The analysis in the previous section suggests that this will understate the relevant differential.

A New Estimate

The interest cost savings due to tax exemption can now be estimated and compared with the revenue foregone. Specifically, we shall seek an incremental figure, as Robinson did—that is, the increase in the interest cost on the gross issues of a single year if these issues had been sold at the alternative (without exemption) yields suggested by the earlier discussion.

A sample of 202 issues stratified by credit category was selected from the total of 6,573 new issues in 1960.[3] The detailed data in this sample were used to estimate the rise in total and annual average interest payments for the sample and by inference for the population. Before presenting the results, first consider the problems of estimating the interest cost increase from the data available and the methods employed. As an illustration, we have taken a serial issue and estimated the effect on interest cost of dropping the exemption feature. Details of the issue are in Table 10.

Conceptually, the objective is to insert the estimated alternative (without exemption) yield curve in place of the one which prevailed when the particular issue was sold. This would indicate the amount by which each serial coupon rate, and thus total interest payments, would rise over the life of the issue to get the same total revenue or "production." Each coupon would have to be raised by approximately the same number of basis points as the rise in the offering yield on that particular serial to get the same production from that serial.[4]

Unfortunately, the information available on the IBA punch-card record of new issues does not provide all of the data needed to make such an estimate. For each issue, the IBA series gives the amount of the issue (par value, denoted by P_t), the weighted average maturity (M), the net interest cost (I), the life of the issue (N) and the syndicate purchase price (R), which is "production" minus the syndicate's gross profit. From this, the total and average annual

[3] The basic data on gross issues of state and local debt and details concerning each issue were made available by the Investment Bankers Association.

[4] The text statement is substantially correct for the range of observed data on municipal yields but does not hold in general. An example will illustrate the error introduced. Consider a serial issue which includes (1) deep discount 25-year bonds with a 1 percent coupon rate selling to yield 3.5 percent and (2) a 1-year bond with a 4 percent coupon selling to yield 1 percent. Now suppose yields on both bonds rise by $1\frac{1}{2}$ percentage points. If the coupon rates are raised by $1\frac{1}{2}$ percentage points in each case, the revenue from the 25-year bond will be 10 percent greater than before and that from the 1 year bond will be less than $\frac{1}{2}$ percent less than before. Note that the errors are in opposite directions but not of equal magnitude.

TABLE 10. Computation of Net Interest Cost for a Hypothetical State or Local Government Bond 15-Year Issue

Maturing in (Years)	Amount (par)	Coupon Rate	Offering Yield	Production	Interest Payments (3)×(2)×(1)	Year Times Amount Outstanding (1)×(2)
(1)	(2)	(3)	(4)	(5)	(6)	(7)
1	$ 1,300,000	5.00%	1.75%	100.24	$ 65,000	$ 1,300,000
2	300,000	5.00	2.00	105.85	30,000	600,000
3	300,000	5.00	2.20	108.09	45,000	900,000
4	300,000	5.00	2.35	110.06	60,000	1,200,000
5	300,000	5.00	2.50	111.68	75,000	1,500,000
6	1,300,000	5.00	2.65	112.96	390,000	7,800,000
7	1,300,000	5.00	2.80	113.90	455,000	9,100,000
8	1,300,000	3.00	2.90	100.71	312,000	10,400,000
9	1,300,000	3.00	3.00	100.00	351,000	11,700,000
10	1,300,000	3.00	3.05	99.57	390,000	13,000,000
11	1,300,000	3.1	3.10	100.00	443,300	14,300,000
12	1,300,000	3.1	3.15	99.45	483,600	15,600,000
13	1,300,000	3.2	3.20	100.00	540,800	16,900,000
14	1,100,000	3.25	3.30	99.44	500,500	15,400,000
15	1,000,000	3.375	3.40	99.71	506,250	15,000,000
	$15,000,000			102.978	$4,647,450	$134,700,000

Dollar "Production" ($=102.978 \times \$15,000,000$) $15,446,700$[a]

(Less) "Spread"   346,700[b]

(Equals) Syndicate Purchase Price   15,100,000

(Less) Premium   100,000[c]

(Equals) Par Amount of Issue $15,000,000

$$\text{Net Interest Cost} = \frac{\$4,647,450 - 100,000}{\$\ 134,700,000} = 3.376\%$$

Average Weighted Maturity $= 8.98$ years

$$\left(= 1\frac{13}{150} + 2\frac{3}{150} + \ldots 15\frac{10}{150} \right)$$

[a] Production is the total revenue to the syndicate (given by coupon for each serial and market yield for that serial) stated as a percentage of par. The production for each serial is multiplied by the par amount of each serial; the products are then summed for all serials, and the ratio of this total to the par amount of the entire issue is the total production figure at the bottom of column (5).

[b] Spread is the difference between production and what the issuing authority receives or, the syndicate's gross profit.

[c] Premium or Discount represents the excess (or deficit) of the purchase price over par value of the issue.

interest payments for any issue can be computed. Denoting the amount maturing in years, 1, 2, .., N as P_1, P_2, .., P_N, and the corresponding coupon rates as C_1, C_2, .., C_N, the amount outstanding times years outstanding, for each serial and in the aggregate (O) is

$$O = 1P_1 + 2P_2 + \cdots + NP_N \quad\cdots\cdots\cdots\cdots\cdots\cdots\cdots\cdots\cdots\cdots(1)$$

$$M = 1\frac{P_1}{P_t} + 2\frac{P_2}{P_t} + \cdots + N\frac{P_N}{P_t} = \frac{O}{P_t} \quad\cdots\cdots\cdots\cdots\cdots\cdots\cdots(2)$$

Net interest cost as commonly computed is

$$I = \frac{1(C_1 P_1) + 2(C_2 P_2) + \cdots + N(C_N P_N) - E}{O} \quad\cdots\cdots\cdots(3)$$

where E represents any premium, that is, $R - P_t$. The numerator here is the sum of total interest payments, less premiums. Denote the numerator as Y.

Then $Y = OI$. Substituting (2) gives

$$Y = P_t MI. \quad\cdots\cdots\cdots\cdots\cdots\cdots\cdots\cdots\cdots(4)$$

Since Y denotes total interest payments minus premiums, that is, $A - E$,

$$A = P_t MI + E \quad\cdots\cdots\cdots\cdots\cdots\cdots\cdots(5)$$

and $\dfrac{A}{N}$ is the average annual interest payment on the issue.

To arrive at the total interest payments on the 202 issues in the sample, multiply the amount (par value) times average maturity times net interest cost and add premiums for each issue, as shown in equation (5). The sum of these calculations for each of the 202 issues is the total interest payment for the sample as a whole.

For a numerical example of this calculation, refer again to Table 10.

$$A = P_t MI + E$$
$$= \$15{,}000{,}000 \times 8.98 \times 0.03376 + \$100{,}000$$
$$= \$4{,}647{,}472$$

which differs from the actual \$4,647,450 only because of rounding of net interest cost (I). The average annual interest payment over the life of the issue is

$$\frac{A}{N} = \frac{\$4{,}647{,}472}{15} = \$309{,}831.47$$

Assume for the moment that yields at all maturities in the alternative yield series are higher than the corresponding yields with the exemption by the same number of basis points. In this case, all coupon rates and net interest cost (I) will rise by the same amount in basis points, namely:

$$\Delta I = \frac{\Delta CP_1 + 2(\Delta CP_2) + \cdots + N(\Delta CP_N)}{O},$$

$$= \frac{\Delta C(P_1 + 2P_2 + \cdots + NP_N)}{O} \text{ which by (1) above}$$

$$= \Delta C.$$

Let Δr = the change in yield. From above, Δr approximately = ΔC. To obtain the increase in total interest payments due to higher offering yields without the exemption, we take the first difference of equation (5) $A = P_t MI + E$ and substitute $\Delta r \doteq \Delta C = \Delta I$.

$$\Delta A = \Delta r P_t M.$$

The increase in average annual interest payments would be $\dfrac{\Delta A}{N}$.

What effect will the flattening of the municipal bond yield curve have on the calculation? As noted in the previous chapter yields on the shorter maturities can be expected to rise by a greater absolute amount than the long-term differential just employed. This makes the increase in total interest cost greater than that just obtained, for we assumed yields in all maturities rose by the same basis points amount. The question is: How much greater is the rise in interest payments?

Note that two effects are compounded. The level of the yield curve changes by equal basis point amounts at all maturities, as just noted. Simultaneously, the slope of the yield curve changes, causing some additional increase in interest costs. We seek to measure the amount by which the change in slope (at the before removal yield levels) will raise interest costs and to add this sum to the estimated cost of the change in level.

As an extreme case, assume that after removal of the exemption feature, the yield curve on municipals becomes perfectly horizontal. This implies that the yield to maturity is independent of the number of years to maturity. Since the rise in long-term yields has been measured previously, the upward sloping yield curve will be rotated through the long-term yield until the curve is flat. The net interest cost computed from the old yield curve is known. Net interest cost with the new, horizontal curve will be approximately higher than the old net interest cost by the difference between the long-term yield on municipals and the old net interest cost figure. This is shown for a hypothetical issue in Table 11.

For this particular issue, net interest cost is 2.66 percent with the upward-sloping yield curve. Now the curve becomes completely flat at the long-term rate, that is, yields in all maturities are now 2.9 percent per annum. The flattening effect causes a rise in net interest cost from 2.66 percent to 2.9 percent in this extreme case.

If all issues were like the example, the effect of a change in slope could be measured very closely by comparing the average long-term rate to average net interest cost before the change. However, the bulk of state-local issues differ from the illustration in one important respect—the coupon structure does not generally parallel the

TABLE 11. Computation of Net Interest Cost of a Hypothetical State or Local Government 10-Year Bond Issue

Maturing in (years)	Amount	Coupon Rate	Offering Yield	Produc- tion	Total Interest Payments (3)×(1)×(2)	Year Times Amount Outstanding (2)×(1)
(1)	(2)	(3)	(4)	(5)	(6)	(7)
1	$ 1,000,000	2.0%	2.0%	100.00	$ 20,000	$ 1,000,000
2	2,000,000	2.1	2.1	100.00	84,000	4,000,000
3	3,000,000	2.2	2.2	100.00	198,000	9,000,000
4	4,000,000	2.3	2.3	100.00	368,000	16,000,000
5	4,000,000	2.4	2.4	100.00	480,000	20,000,000
6	4,000,000	2.5	2.5	100.00	600,000	24,000,000
7	5,000,000	2.6	2.6	100.00	910,000	35,000,000
8	5,000,000	2.7	2.7	100.00	1,080,000	40,000,000
9	6,000,000	2.8	2.8	100.00	1,512,000	54,000,000
10	6,000,000	2.9	2.9	100.00	1,740,000	60,000,000
	$40,000,000			100.00	$6,992,000	$263,000,000

$$\text{Net Interest Cost} = \frac{\$ 6,992,000}{\$263,000,000} = 2.66\%$$

offering yield curve. Generally speaking, the coupon structures are "flatter," that is, the coupons are often set high in the early maturities and low in the later maturities. As Robinson has shown,[5] this lowers the net interest cost computed by municipal finance officers since the latter generally do not make calculations on a present value basis. If the net interest cost figure is compared with the long-term yield, the rise in net interest cost resulting from the flatter yield curve will be overstated. Net interest cost for a flat yield curve will be less than the long-term yield. Moreover, comparing average net interest cost and average long-term yields will also overstate the effects of the change in slope to the extent that there are issues whose longest serial maturity is less than that for the long-term rate used, that is, twenty years.

The available data do not permit an estimate which avoids these elements of overstatement. For 1960, a comparison by credit category of average net interest cost (for the sample) and average long-term yields (IBA) on municipals suggests that complete flattening of the yield curves on these issues would have raised net interest cost some 25 basis points at most.

Put differently, the assumption that yields in all maturities rise by 25 basis points is equivalent to the effect of a horizontal yield curve. But this is an unlikely extreme for several reasons. First, it is quite unlikely that yields in the one- to five-year range would rise to equal the long-term yield as this presumes. Further, the extreme is itself an overstatement both because of the coupon structure effect and because some issues do not have long maturities. Finally, some issues have serial maturities of more than twenty years. Yields on the longest maturities will fall when the slope of the curve becomes horizontal, if the same assumptions are retained.

Eighteen basis points are allowed for the flattening effect, a judgment which appears to be generous. The previous range for the long-term yield differential was 101-184 basis points. This raises the range to 119-202 basis points.[6]

The net interest cost for each of the sample issues can now be increased by 119 and 202 basis points to obtain an estimate of the

[5] Robinson, *op. cit.*, App. B., pp. 217-23.

[6] This analysis of the effect of a flattening of the term structure was added to the original background paper after helpful discussion on this point at the Experts' Conference. (See pp. 116 ff.)

maximum and minimum increase in total and average annual interest payments, as was done in the illustrative issue. Summary information on the characteristics of the sample and results of the calculated interest cost increase is provided in Table 12. The 202 sample issues represented 3.07 percent of the total number of issues in 1960, and the $220.6 million of issues in the sample was also 3.07 percent of the population dollar total. For total issues, the arithmetic average size was $1,094, and the sample arithmetic mean was $1,092. For the sample, total interest payments were $109.5 million and the total annual average interest payments $4.9 million (Table 13). If these figures are blown up to approximate the same variables for the population as a whole, aggregate total interest payments for the life of the bonds of $3.4 billion and a total annual average of $148.9 million per year are suggested.

Table 13 gives the information on the rise in total and annual average interest payments, suggested by the two alternative yield series. Increasing net interest cost for each sample issue by the minimum 119 and maximum 202 basis point differentials raises total interest payments on the same volume of sample issues by $33.8 million and $57.7 million respectively. Annual average interest payments rise by $1.5 million in the minimum case and by $2.6 million at the maximum, or 30.7 percent and 53.5 percent, respectively.

TABLE 12. Comparison of Characteristics of All State and Local Government Bond Issues in 1960 and 202 Issues in Study Sample

(Dollar items in thousands)

Rating	Population			Sample		
	Number of Issues	Amount	Average Size	Number of Issues	Amount	Average Size
Aaa	237	$ 762,612	$3,218	8	$ 17,524	$2,190
Aa	600	1,566,420	2,611	18	46,125	2,563
A	1,111	2,074,303	1,867	34	64,607	1,900
Baa	644	755,662	1,173	20	28,087	1,404
Ba[a]	66	66,168	1,003	2	1,750	875
Unrated	3,915	1,965,397	502	120	62,525	521
Total	6,573	$7,193,382	$1,094	202	$220,618	$1,092

[a] Includes 2 "B" issues.

TABLE 13. Summary of Interest Payment Data Calculated for Sample Issues

(*In thousands*)

Rating	Total Interest Payments	Average Annual Interest Payments	Estimated Rise in Total Interest Payments		Estimated Rise in Annual Interest Payments	
			Minimum	Maximum	Minimum	Maximum
Aaa	$ 6,722	$ 284	$ 2,558	$ 4,364	$ 108	$ 184
Aa	22,839	952	7,583	12,935	319	545
A	25,274	1,340	8,024	13,688	398	729
Baa	16,246	655	4,873	8,313	198	338
Ba	1,094	48	287	489	13	22
Unrated	37,314	1,570	10,499	17,909	454	774
Totals	$109,488	$4,894	$33,824	$57,699	$1,491	$2,592

When the sample results are applied to the aggregate of issues in 1960, they suggest that total interest payments on 1960 gross issues would have been higher by a minimum of $1 billion and a maximum of $1.8 billion. Annual average interest payments would have risen from $45.7 to $79.5 million. This assumes, of course, that the same total volume of issues would have been floated at the higher levels of interest rates. Although this is unlikely to be true, correction for the error introduced by this assumption requires an estimate of the elasticity of supply with respect to interest rates and is well beyond the scope of this study.

The meaning of these figures to the present study can be suggested apart from the dollar magnitudes involved. Let average annual interest payments be 30.7 to 53.5 percent higher, as the sample suggests. The increase in federal revenues resulting from taxation of the interest on these issues would have to be between

$$23.5 \left(\frac{30.7}{130.7} \times 100 \right) \text{ and } 34.9 \left(\frac{53.5}{153.5} \times 100 \right)$$

percent of annual interest payments before the revenue gain to the Treasury exceeds the increased interest cost borne by state and local governments. How much the added tax yield would be relative to annual interest payments (without exemption) is the subject of the following chapter.

CHAPTER V

Revenue Implications

THE TAXATION OF INTEREST payments on new issues of state and local bonds will result in higher interest payments as discussed in the previous chapter. We now seek a measure of the revenue yield to the federal government from taxing the higher level of interest payments. We again look at problems encountered in earlier efforts, and then attempt a new estimate.

Problems of Earlier Estimates

The difficulties of estimating the revenue loss are at least as complex as those involved in estimating the interest cost saving. First, some sort of "average marginal" tax rates must be estimated for the various recipients of tax-exempt interest income. More important, it is not reasonable to assume an unchanged distribution of new taxable issues among investor groups should the exemption be removed. Some hypothesis concerning the distribution of purchases of state and local debt without the exemption feature must be developed and used.

The problem of "average marginal" rates is not insoluble. Usable estimates have been developed for the one difficult group—individuals.[1] No extensive treatment has been given to the distribu-

---

[1] See Roland I. Robinson, *Postwar Market for State and Local Government Securities* (National Bureau of Economic Research, 1960), p. 192.

tion problem. Most studies have used the existing distribution.[2] A few have recognized the existence of the problem.

Robinson attempted to provide for the changed distribution of securities in making estimates of incremental revenue gains. He estimated the revenue loss as the average marginal tax rate times annual interest income (yield times amount invested) on a similar investment in taxable securities. For banks and other corporations, the taxable securities are assumed to be bonds. He assumed that individuals would invest in corporate bonds and/or corporate stock.

Of course, this does not account for all of the distribution shift. Particularly, it does not reallocate the bonds which individuals and banks no longer buy. It makes no allowance for purchases by life insurance companies, mutual savings banks, and pension funds and the taxation of the interest income at their "average marginal" tax rates. Although Robinson recognized the importance of the distribution problem in assuming alternative investments by individuals and banks, his procedure failed to capture the full effect of the changed security distribution. The revenue estimate can be improved by allowing at least roughly for the other shifts suggested.

A New Estimate

Assume that the volume of both total security issues and issues of state and local bonds are unchanged after the exemption is dropped. Let yields on municipals equal average yields elsewhere. Further assume that each investor buys the same mix of new security issues that he would have purchased if exemption remained in effect. Then the maximum tax revenue due to imposing the income tax on interest from state and local bonds is given by multiplying the average marginal tax rate applicable to those who buy

[2] For example, Harley L. Lutz, "The Fiscal and Economic Aspects of the Taxation of Public Securities," reprinted in *Taxation of Government Securities and Salaries,* Hearings before the Senate Special Committee on Taxation of Government Securities and Salaries, 76 Cong. 1 sess. (1939), pp. 114-22; Vance N. Kirby, "State and Local Bond Interest," House Committee on Ways and Means, *Tax Revision Compendium,* Vol. 1 (1959), pp. 679-80; Harvey E. Brazer, "Interest on State and Local Bonds and the Federal Income Tax," *ibid.,* p. 725; James A. Maxwell, "Exclusion from Income of Interest on State and Local Government Obligations," *ibid.,* p. 712.

municipals before the exemption is dropped by aggregate interest payments on taxable municipals.

A similar conclusion can be reached with an alternative set of assumptions. It is presented to illustrate the issue and the importance of the analysis which follows for a proper appraisal of the revenue obtained from the tax. Assume that there are no tax shelters over investment in other securities. Again let the volume of new flotations remain unchanged and let yields on municipals equal average yields elsewhere. Now assume that each investor purchases a mix of new issues which maximizes his after-tax return. Whatever the mix of securities purchased by those who formerly bought municipals, their tax payments will be the same as if they bought newly issued municipals after the exemption is removed. The switch into municipals by those who would have bought other taxable securities will produce no change in the tax yield from them. The increase in tax yield will again equal the average marginal rates of present investors times the interest paid on newly issued taxable municipals. Portfolio changes will alter the revenue collected only if alternative tax shelters are available.

This is illustrated in the following example. Consider two groups of investors, (A) buys municipal securities which yield 4 percent with exemption and (B) buys "taxable" securities that yield 5 percent. Interest on these securities is taxed at average marginal tax rates of 50 percent and 20 percent, respectively. Then the interest incomes and tax yields with exemption would have been:

	Municipals Group (A)	Taxables Group (B)
Purchases...................	$400	$500
Yield......................	0.04	0.05
Interest....................	$16.00	$25.00
Marginal tax rate...........	0.5	0.2
Tax yield...................	0 (tax-exempt)	$ 5.00

The tax yield is $5.00. Now suppose the exemption is not available and the municipals group switches $200 to taxables and the taxables group $200 to municipals and yields on both types of securities are now 5 percent.

	Municipals		Taxables	
	(A)	(B)	(A)	(B)
Purchases.........	$200	$200	$200	$300
Yield.............	0.05	0.05	0.05	0.05
Interest...........	$10.00	$10.00	$10.00	$15.00
Marginal tax rate...	0.5	0.2	0.5	0.2
Tax yield.........	$ 5.00	$ 2.00	$ 5.00	$ 3.00

The tax yield rises to $15.00. The increase in revenue of $10.00 equals the after-removal interest payments on municipals ($20.00) times the average marginal tax rate (0.5) applicable to those buying municipals before removal. More generally, if the volume of securities floated is unchanged,

Let S = market value of state-local securities

X = market value of alternative investments that those who hold S when tax exempt acquire if S becomes taxable

bS = amount of switching from S to X

r_1 = yield of S with tax exemption

r_2 = yield of S without tax exemption

r_3 = yield of X when S is tax exempt

r_4 = yield of X when S is taxable

t_1 = marginal tax rate for those who hold S when S is tax exempt

t_2 = marginal tax rate for those who hold X when S is tax exempt

a = tax shelter factor for X, the fraction of regular tax rates applicable to interest from X, assumed to be constant.

With S exempt, the government's revenue is $t_2 r_3 aX$. With S taxable, holders of S will exchange S for X. The government's revenue, R, will be:

$$R = r_4 t_1 abS + r_2 t_1 (1 - b)S + t_2 r_2 (bS) + t_2 r_4 a(X - bS). \cdots\cdots\cdots (1)$$

The gain in revenue will be

$$\Delta R = r_4 t_1 abS + r_2 t_1 (1 - b)S + t_2 r_2 (bS) + t_2 r_4 a(X - bS) - t_2 r_3 aX. \quad (2)$$

If $r_3 = r_4$, this reduces to

$$S[r_4ab(t_1 - t_2) + r_2(t_1 + b[t_2 - t_1])]$$
$$= bS[(t_1 - t_2)(ar_4 - r_2)] + r_2t_1S. \cdots \cdots (3)$$

And, in our example, where there is no tax shelter, $(a = 1)$, if $r_2 = r_3 = r_4 = r$, this becomes

$$Sr(t_1) \cdots \cdots \cdots \cdots \cdots \cdots \cdots \cdots \cdots \cdots \cdots \cdots \cdots (4)$$

Thus, if there is no alternative tax shelter, the tax revenue gained is independent of the portfolio redistribution. All values of b yield the same tax as noted above.

For any value of a other than $a = 1$, some alternative tax shelter is available.

Equation (3) shows that the additional tax collections depend on both a and b. Rearranging terms,

$$\Delta R = bS[r(a - 1)(t_1 - t_2)] + rt_1S. \cdots \cdots \cdots \cdots (5)$$

In the extreme case, where there is a complete tax shelter available to bondholders, $a = 0$. The government collects no tax revenue from bondholders before exemption is removed. If $r_2 = r_3 = r_4 = r$, exemption removal yields revenue

$$\Delta R = rS[(1 - b)t_1 + bt_2] \cdots \cdots \cdots \cdots \cdots (6)$$

dependent on a weighted average of the two tax rates. If investors acquire the same portfolios before and after the exemption is removed, equations (6) and (4) produce the same addition to revenue. At the other extreme, if $b = 1$ and $a = 0$,

$$\Delta R = Srt_2.[3] \cdots \cdots \cdots \cdots \cdots \cdots \cdots \cdots \cdots (7)$$

In this case, the increase in tax yield due to dropping the exemption on new issues is equal to the after-removal interest payments on new issues of state and local bonds times the average marginal tax rates paid by new holders of state and local bonds.

Where the actual yield will fall between these extremes will depend on the actual values of a and b, as well as before- and after-removal values of r_2, r_3 and r_4. In the special cases when $a = 1$ and r_2

---

[3] In light of our earlier discussion to the effect that all yields would likely rise if the exemption is removed (i.e., $r_3 \neq r_4$), it is clear that equation (4) understates both the maximum and the minimum tax yield from dropping the exemption. If $r_4 = r_2 \neq r_3$, equation (4) is understated by $(r_4 - r_3)t_2X$. Equation (7) is unchanged and equals r_2t_2S.

TABLE 14. Marginal Tax Rates for Holders of State and Local Securities, December 1960

(*Dollar amounts in billions*)

Investor Group	Amount Held	Percentage Distribution	Average Marginal Tax Rate	(2)×(3)
	(1)	(2)	(3)	(4)
Consumers......................	$27.5	40.5%	60.0%	24.3%
State and local funds..............	7.2	10.6	—	—
Commercial banks	17.6	25.9	52.0	13.5
Mutual savings banks..............	0.7	1.0	—	—
Life insurance companies...........	3.7	5.5	20.5	1.1
Nonlife insurance companies	8.7	12.8	52.0	6.6
Nonfinancial corporations	2.1	3.1	52.0	1.6
Other	0.4	0.6	—	—
Total outstanding	$67.9	100.0	—	47.1%

Sources:
Column (1): *Federal Reserve Bulletin,* August 1961, p. 993.
Column (2): Column (1) divided by total in Column (1).
Column (3): Consumers: Roland I. Robinson, *The Postwar Market for State and Local Government Securities* (National Bureau of Economic Research, 1960) pp. 191–92. Life insurance companies—computed from aggregate industry data. (See pp. 70–71.) Nonlife insurance companies—figure is overstated, applies to stock companies only.

$= r_3 = r_4$, the equation reduces to (4) no matter what the value of b, and when b = 0, it reduces to (4) regardless of the values of a, r_2, r_3, or r_4.[4]

To obtain numerical estimates of the revenue gained from the tax, values must be assigned to a, b, and t. Let us first estimate what the maximum average marginal tax rate on the after-removal interest would be. Assume that present buyers of municipals continue to purchase them after removal and that the applicable rates are their existing marginal rates of tax.[5] Table 14 shows the proportion of outstanding state and local bonds held by the various investor

[4] If the yield on state and local bonds is less than that on the alternative security after exemption removal (i.e., $r_2 < r_4$), the maximum revenue change is no longer given by equation (4), but by equation (3). The maximum average marginal tax rate is no longer t_1, but is given by $t_1 + b(t_2 - t_1)(1 - \frac{r_4}{r_2}a)$. We shall refer to this at a later point in this chapter.

[5] It will be recalled that this is equivalent to the assumption that present buyers of municipals shift into securities with yields that are fully taxable at ordinary rates.

groups, the approximate average marginal tax rate for each group, and the computed weighted average marginal tax rate. The proportion of outstandings held rather than the proportion of new issues purchased was used to allocate the 1960 volume of issues among investor groups. The importance of various investor groups in the market for municipals varies with the business cycle. Using outstandings probably gives a better picture of the "average composition" of investor groups.

The aggregate average marginal tax rates for present holders of municipals suggested by the computation is 47.1 percent. This probably is a slight overestimate, because the average marginal rates used for nonlife and life insurance companies are perhaps a bit high. In any case, however, this does suggest that the maximum marginal tax rate applicable to after-removal state-local interest would be less than 50 percent.

The absolute minimum average marginal tax rate applicable to after-removal interest payment is obtained in equation (7) when $a = 0$, $b = 1$, and $t_2 < t_1$. This means that there is some alternative investment completely free of taxation. Those who purchased exempt municipals shift out of municipals and into alternative shelters. The new purchasers of new municipal issues are induced to abandon their shelters and acquire municipals. In this case, the average marginal tax rate applicable to after-removal interest payments would be that of the after-removal purchasers of municipals, $t_2 < t_1$. The question obviously arises: Who would be the after-removal purchasers of municipals? It was suggested earlier that without exemption the distribution of municipals would parallel that for corporate bonds outstanding. Let us start with that assumption. Then the minimum average marginal rate would be suggested by the weighted average marginal rate applicable to corporate bond interest, if we assume that the groups represented now acquire municipals in place of corporates. We continue to assume that $r_4 = r_2$ and that the volume issued remains unchanged.

Table 15 shows the percentage distribution of corporate bond holdings at the end of 1960. This is the assumed distribution of municipal issues inferred for each investor group. The breakdown illustrates the assumption previously made—without the exemption

TABLE 15. Distribution of Corporate Bonds Outstanding December 31, 1960

Investor Group	Percentage Distribution
Consumers..	14.0%
Non-profit sector...	10.0
State and local trust funds....................................	7.3
Commercial banks..	0.9
Mutual savings banks...	3.6
Life insurance companies......................................	45.0
Nonlife insurance companies...................................	2.7
Pension funds...	13.9
Other..	2.5
Total...	100.0

Source: *Federal Reserve Bulletin*, April 1961, p. 485. Data include foreign as well as domestic corporate bonds. Consumer and non-profit sector separated on the basis of 1955 data. Detail does not add to total due to rounding

feature life insurance companies and pension funds are presumed to be much more active purchasers of municipals. Individuals, though still important, take a smaller proportion.

The next problem is applying suitable average marginal tax rates to the interest received by each investor group. There is such a serious lack of detailed information on this that our estimates must be taken only as rough approximations. For some of the groups, no problem exists: for all practical purposes, the average marginal tax rate is zero for the nonprofit sector, mutual savings banks with relatively small capital funds, pension funds, and state and local trust funds.

For commercial banks and nonlife insurance companies, the 52 percent marginal rate for corporations can be applied. This rate also applies to a few mutual savings banks. It is for the two largest single groups, individuals and life insurance companies, that calculation of average marginal rates becomes particularly difficult.

For individuals, the average marginal tax rate reflects the distribution of corporate bond interest income among investors in the various individual income tax brackets. Individuals who purchase new issues are assumed to be those who hold outstandings in the same brackets and subject to the same marginal rates. The only tangible evidence on the distribution of corporate bond inter-

TABLE 16. Distribution of Corporate Bond Interest and Average
Marginal Tax Rate

Adjusted Gross Income Class	Percentage of Total Interest in Wisconsin	Average Marginal Federal Rate	Col. (1) times Col. (2)
	(1)	(2)	(3)
Below $9,999.........................	70%	21%	14.7%
$10,000–$19,999.....................	16	29	4.6
$20,000–$49,999.....................	11	47	5.2
$50,000 and above...................	4	77	3.0
			———
Average marginal tax rate for corporate bond interest...			27.5%

Sources:
    Column (1): Thomas R. Atkinson, *The Pattern of Financial Asset Ownership; Wisconsin Individuals, 1949*, Table 1, Appendix.
    Column (2): C. Harry Kahn, *Personal Deductions in the Federal Income Tax,* (National Bureau of Economic Research, 1960), p. 155. We used the midpoints of the marginal rates in brackets covered by the wider brackets here. Even if the extreme upper rate is used, the aggregate average rate would rise only to 30.6 percent.

est among individual tax brackets is that compiled by Atkinson in his study of 1949 Wisconsin income tax returns.[6] This is summarized in Table 16. The Wisconsin data show that 70 percent of corporate bond interest income for that year was in adjusted gross income (AGI) classes below $10,000, and 86 percent was in AGI classes below $20,000.[7] If Kahn's average marginal tax rates developed for AGI classes are applied,[8] the Atkinson data suggest an average marginal tax rate for individuals' receipts of corporate bond interest of about 27.5 percent. This rate will be used as the rate applicable to interest on municipal bonds without exemption.

For life insurance companies, estimating an average marginal rate on investment income is made difficult by the complexity of the provisions for taxation in the 1959 law. The tax rate figure commonly cited in the industry is 11 percent. This may be accurate for some purposes but is not strictly applicable to this discussion since it is based on average rather than marginal rates of return.

[6] Thomas R. Atkinson, *The Pattern of Financial Asset Ownership; Wisconsin Individuals, 1949* (National Bureau of Economic Research, 1956), Table 1, App. A.

[7] The AGI on Wisconsin returns includes state and local government bond interest and excludes interest on federal obligations.

[8] C. Harry Kahn, *Personal Deductions in the Federal Income Tax* (National Bureau of Economic Research, 1960), p. 155.

The tax formula for life insurance companies is

$$T_I = t(Y_I - iR) \cdots\cdots\cdots\cdots\cdots\cdots (1)$$

Where T_I is tax on net investment income, Y_I is net investment income in any year, i is the previous five year earning rate on assets, R is total policy reserves at end of a year, and t is the corporate tax rate. This is also

$$T_I = t(rA - iR) \cdots\cdots\cdots\cdots\cdots\cdots (2)$$

where r is the current yield on assets and A the value of assets. If the ratio R/A is given by B, then

$$T_I = tA(r - iB) \cdots\cdots\cdots\cdots\cdots\cdots (3)$$

The marginal tax rate is

$$\frac{\Delta T_I}{\Delta rA} = \frac{t\Delta A(r - iB)}{\Delta Ar} = \frac{t(r - iB)}{r} \cdots\cdots\cdots\cdots\cdots (4)$$

Substituting values of $r = .04$, $i = .0375$, $t = .52$ and $B = .83$ as suggested by aggregate data for the industry[9] we obtain

$$\frac{\Delta T_I}{\Delta rA} = .52 \left(\frac{.00887}{.04000} \right) \times 100 = 11.5 \text{ percent.}$$

Note, however, that r here is the current average yield on assets. We are discussing marginal investments in municipals, which we indicated in the interest cost chapter would yield 4.77 to 5.58 percent on the average,[10] so r for our purposes will have to be higher in consequence. If these rates for r are used, we obtain

$$\frac{\Delta T_I}{\Delta rA} = 18 \text{ to } 23 \text{ percent.}$$

Putting together the average marginal tax rates for each investor group and the hypothetical distribution of gross issues previously developed, a weighted average marginal tax rate for without-exemption "municipal" bond interest of 13.9 to 16.2 percent is obtained, as Table 17 shows. This range is the effective not the absolute minimum. It will be recalled that the absolute minimum was t_2, the weighted average marginal tax rate for after-removal purchasers of municipals, when the shift was a complete one, that is,

[9] Institute of Life Insurance, *Life Insurance Fact Book* (1960), pp. 57 and 61.

[10] This is based on the average yields on rated municipals in 1960 plus the differential of 1.19 to 2.02 percentage points suggested in the previous chapter.

TABLE 17. Minimum Weighted Average Marginal Tax Rate on Municipal
Bond Interest, Assuming Removal of Federal Tax Exemption,
December 1960

Investor Group	Assumed Proportion of New Issues Purchased	Average Marginal Tax Rates	Col. (1) Times Col. (2)
	(1)	(2)	(3)
Individuals.......................	14.0%	27.5%	3.8%
Nonprofit sector.................	10.0	—	—
State and local trust funds........	7.3	—	—
Commercial banks...............	0.9	52.0	0.5
Mutual savings banks............	3.6	—	—
Life insurance companies.........	45.0	18.0–23.0	8.1–10.4
Nonlife insurance companies.......	2.7	52.0	1.4
Pension funds...................	13.9	—	—
Other.........................	2.5	—	—
Total.......................	100.0		13.8–16.1

Source:
   Column (1): Table 15.
   Column (2): Explained in text.

when b = 1 and a = 0. A comparison of Tables 14 and 17 shows, on
the assumption that after-removal purchases parallel those for corporate bonds, that the present purchasers of municipal securities
would not shift out of them completely. Individuals would continue to take some 14 percent of gross issues (though perhaps not
the same individuals with the same average marginal tax rates). Life
insurance companies and state and local trust funds will hold some
municipals with or without exemption. However, the figure is suggestive of what the minimum effective rate could be.

Where the actual average marginal rate will fall between the
47 percent maximum and the 14-16 percent minimum is the crucial
question. It is unlikely that the applicable rate will be at either extreme. There will be some shifting, and it will probably lower the
weighted average marginal rate applicable to after-removal state
and local interest payments. This will reduce the additional tax
yield from dropping the exemption.[11]

The extent to which shifting takes place depends on the supply

[11] Note that the shift we refer to is one where investors are adjusting the way they
allocate future investment flows. There will also be a readjustment of existing portfolios—a stock adjustment—which we have not treated here.

of alternative sources of tax-exemption as noted earlier. For present analysis, we are concerned with new issues of securities. These are small relative to outstanding securities. This fact has important implications for the effective after-removal average marginal tax rate, since the removal of one form of exemption leads to more intensive use of alternative forms. In the short run, most of the existing forms of exemption are relatively fixed in supply. Those for whom exemption is most profitable will bid up the price of the remaining exemptions and thus induce a redistribution of security purchases by investors. As time passes, an increased supply of exempt, or partially exempt, securities will be forthcoming.

Capital market specialists have suggested some of the likely portfolio changes. They speak particularly of a shift into equities by individuals in the high tax brackets and nonlife insurance companies. They suggest that these groups would be replaced in the market for new issues of municipals by life insurance companies and pension funds, both with much lower marginal tax rates. This presumes that the latter two institutional investors would reduce their purchases of equities to buy more of the then taxable municipals. In effect they would trade their use of the tax shelter on equities to those in the higher brackets who would benefit more from it.

It is clear that the revenue obtained from the tax depends on the rate of purchase by the various investor groups. Precise rates cannot be forecast. However, to gauge the effect of this general shift on the average marginal tax rate applicable without the exemption feature, some indication of the magnitude of shift involved is needed. Assume the difference between the distribution of municipals with exemption and the present distribution of corporate bonds measures the shift. Table 18 compares the percentage distribution of holdings of these two types of securities at the end of 1960. This comparison suggests a shift of about 66 percent of gross issues. Principally, this reflects large declines for individuals, commercial banks, and nonlife insurance companies and sizable increases for life insurance companies, pension funds, and nonprofit institutions.

However, this estimate of the alternative allocation of new taxable municipals overstates the percentage changes. First, commer-

TABLE 18. Distribution of Corporate and State-Local Government Bonds, December 31, 1960

Investor Group	Percentage of Exempt Municipals Held	Percentage of Corporate Bonds Held	Percentage Points Shift
	(1)	(2)	(3)
Individuals.....................	40.5%	14.0%	−26.5%
Nonprofit sector................	—	10.0	+10.1
State and local funds...........	10.6	7.3	− 3.3
Commercial banks...............	25.9	0.9	−25.0
Mutual savings banks............	1.0	3.6	+ 2.6
Life insurance companies.........	5.5	45.0	+39.5
Nonlife insurance companies.......	12.8	2.7	−10.1
Pension funds...................	—	13.9	+13.9
Others.........................	3.8	2.5	− 1.3
Total.......................	100.0	100.0	±66.2

Sources:
Column (1): Table 14.
Column (2): Table 15.
Column (3): Column (2) less column (1).
Columns may not add to total due to rounding.

cial banks would absorb a much larger proportion of new issues of state and local bonds than the figure of 0.9 percent used. They buy such securities for liquidity reasons as well as after-tax yield. If issuing governments continue to offer short-term serials, banks would be unlikely to substitute some liquid asset for state and local bonds. Recall from above that the yields on shorter maturities of the state-local securities might rise by 100 to 200 basis points. In these circumstances, bankers would probably prefer high-yield state-local securities to intermediate federal debt or some comparable security. Although the present tax advantage of state-local securities provides strong reasons for holding them, it does not follow that loss of the tax exemption would cause commercial banks to shift completely into assets sheltered by other tax "loopholes." Few are available to them. Moreover, there are the deposit and public relations ties locally which would encourage them to continue purchasing municipals. Finally, banks would still buy municipals because these are the only securities in which they can act as underwriters.

It also seems unlikely that life insurance companies would purchase 45 percent of the new issues. This implies gross purchases

TABLE 19. Distribution of Purchases of Municipals and Final Assumed
Distribution without the Exemption Feature

Investor Group	Percentage of Purchases with Exemption	Assumed Percentage of Purchases without Exemption
	(1)	(2)
Individuals..............................	40.5	14.0
Nonprofit sector.........................	—	10.1
State and local funds....................	10.6	20.0
Commercial banks........................	25.9	10.0
Mutual savings banks....................	1.0	3.6
Life insurance companies.................	5.5	23.2
Nonlife insurance companies..............	12.8	2.7
Pension funds...........................	—	13.9
Others..................................	3.8	2.5
Total...............................	100.0	100.0

Sources:
    Column (1): Table 18.
    Column (2): Column (1) adjusted as explained.
    Columns may not add to totals due to rounding.

in 1960 of roughly $3 billion, almost a third of the gross flows of
funds through life insurance companies in recent years.[12] Such a
massive concentration of their total gross flows on state and local
securities hardly seems reasonable.

Finally, the comparison surely errs in suggesting that state and
local government trust funds would take a smaller proportion of
issues without the exemption. Table 18 shows that they presently
hold more than 10 percent of the outstanding issues. Removal of
the exemption feature raises the effective yield on state-local issues
for these tax-exempt institutions. Doubtless they would increase,
rather than decrease, their rate of purchase.

An alternative estimate of the distribution without exemption
has been made, using lower purchase proportions for life insurance
companies and correspondingly higher ones for commercial banks
and state and local trust funds. Specifically, we assume that, with-

[12] See Kenneth M. Wright, "Gross Flows of Funds Through Life Insurance Companies," *Journal of Finance,* Vol. 15 (May 1960), pp. 140-56. It would be desirable to
check gross investment funds available against implied gross purchases of municipals
for each investor group. Unfortunately, data on gross flows are available only for
life insurance companies.

out the exemption feature, (1) state-local funds would about double their proportion of issues purchased (to 20 percent)[13] and commercial banks would buy about 10 percent of gross issues, (2) the gains of these two would be the counterpart of a lower purchase proportion for life insurance companies, and (3) other investors would acquire municipals in the proportion that they now hold corporate bonds. These changes should improve the previous approximation, though the supporting evidence is admittedly based on qualitative judgment. The resulting assumed final distribution of purchases is shown and compared with the present distribution in Table 19. The total shift of more than 53 percentage points would then appear as follows:

Shifts into Municipals (Percent of gross issues)		Shifts Out of Municipals (Percent of gross issues)	
Life insurance companies	17.7	Individuals	26.5
Pension funds	13.9	Commercial banks	15.9
State and local funds	9.4	Nonlife insurance companies	10.1
Nonprofit organizations	10.1	Others	1.3
Mutual savings banks	2.6		

What effect will such shifts have on the maximum weighted average marginal tax rate? Assume individuals and nonlife insurance companies (Group I) shift from municipals into equities, and that commercial banks (Group III) shift into corporate bonds. Assume that life insurance companies, pension funds, the nonprofit sector, state-local funds, and mutual savings banks (Group II), in shifting into municipals, forego the equities that individuals and nonlife insurance companies take and the corporate bonds that commercial banks take. Let gross issues be S and the proportion involved in the shift b. Let c be the proportion of the shift (bS) represented by the shift of commercial banks from municipal bonds to corporate bonds. Using these symbols, the shifting is summed up as follows:

[13] As of December 31, 1960, state and local trust funds held some $35.3 billion of credit and equity market instruments, of which $17.6 billion were U. S. Government securities, $7.2 billion were state-local bonds, and $7.8 billion were corporate bonds. (Data from *Federal Reserve Bulletin,* April 1961, p. 484.) If gross new issues are at an annual rate of $8 billion, they would acquire $1.6 billion per year.

Investor Group	Municipals	Corporates	Equities	All Securities
Group I	$-(1-c)bS$	0	$+(1-c)bS$	0
Group II	$+bS$	$-cbS$	$-(1-c)bS$	0
Group III	$-cbS$	$+cbS$	0	0
Total	0	0	0	0

Denote the weighted average marginal tax rates of the three groups as t_1, t_2, and t_3, respectively. Call the after-removal yields on municipals r_2, after-removal yields on corporate bonds r_3, and after-removal yields on equities r_e. Finally, let a_1 be the "tax shelter factor" applicable to the return on equities for those shifting from municipals to equities and let a_2 be the shelter factor for those acquiring equities in place of municipals. Then the effect of the shift on the maximum weighted average marginal tax rate applicable to after-removal municipal interest payments is given by

$$\Delta t_a = \frac{a_1 t_1 r_e(1-c)bS - t_1 r_2(1-c)bS + t_2 r_2 bS - t_2 a_2 r_e(1-c)bS - t_2 r_3 cbS - t_3 r_2 cbS + t_3 r_3 cbS}{Sr_2}$$

Where $r_2 = r_3$, this reduces to

$$\Delta t_a = b(1-c)\left[t_2 - t_1 - \frac{r_e}{r_2}(a_2 t_2 - a_1 t_1)\right].$$

The following values for the "t's" are suggested by the average marginal tax rates in Tables 14 and 17 and weights implicit in the distribution of securities just discussed.

$$t_1 = 0.58$$
$$t_2 = 0.07$$
$$t_3 = 0.52$$

The value of c, again using our illustrative shift data, would be

$$0.30\left(= \frac{15.9}{53.7}\right).$$

The data presented earlier on the interest cost saving suggested that the after-removal rise in yields of municipals would be from 1.19 to 2.02 percentage points; in 1960, this would have meant average yields on new issues of municipals, r_2 of 4.77 to 5.58 percent. A separate calculation can be made for Δt_a using each of these as the values for r_2.

The major remaining problems are to determine r_e—returns on investment in equities—and the "a's", the tax shelter factors applicable to r_e. Returns on investment in equities consist of dividend receipts and realized capital gains. The types of equities, with different ratios of dividend to capital gains returns, involved in the shift are not known. Since the shift is large, we will use an average value for r_e. The dividend portion, taken from Standard and Poor's average dividend/price ratio, averaged 3.48 percent in 1960. The difficult problem, both conceptually and statistically, is the capital gains portion of r_e. Note that we are referring here to the capital gains yield that investors who purchase municipals instead of equities will realize in an average future year. No attempt is made to estimate the present value of tax receipts from capital gains which remain unrealized at the end of the year.

One rough way of gauging the revenue yield from capital gains is to look back at the rise in stock prices over a previous period and assume that the per annum rate of increase in stock prices represents the average per annum rate of capital gains likely on the shares acquired after the tax is enacted. This can then be adjusted to a realized basis by assuming that the ratio of the value of stocks traded on the New York Stock Exchange to the average value of stocks listed is an indicator of the ratio of realized to accrued capital gains in any year since it roughly suggests the average length of time shares are held.

The rate of accrued capital gains return is here taken to be the per annum rate of increase of Standard and Poor's composite stock price index for the ten years ending December 1960. The index went from an average of 22.34 (1941-43 = 10) in 1951 to an average of 55.85 in 1960, a compound rate of growth of 9.9 percent. The data on value of stocks traded to average value listed on the New York Exchange remained in a range of 10-20 percent in the 1950's. Using 0.15 as the ratio of accrued to realized capital gains, the return on equities relevant to the tax problem, then, becomes

$$r_e = 0.15(0.099) + 0.0348 = 0.04965.$$

Now a, the tax-shelter factor for the return on equities, is different for the capital gains and dividend portion of returns on equities and different in each case for the two groups changing their acquisitions. The dividend credit provision applies only to individuals. It provides a tax shelter which changes inversely with income and tax bracket. For the upper brackets, however, it is a relatively minor tax shelter and provides a relatively small reduction of the marginal tax applicable. It will be ignored in this discussion. The capital gains tax shelter factor is in practice unity for life insurance companies, pension funds, and the nonprofit sector, that is, there is no practical lowering of the marginal rate applicable to capital gains income relative to other income. Life insurance companies pay a higher marginal rate on capital gains (25 percent) than on net investment income, and the latter two groups have for all practical purposes zero marginal tax rates for all forms of income; a_2 is therefore taken as unity.

For individuals the tax shelter factor for capital gains is 0.5 up to $18,000 taxable income for an individual and up to $36,000 taxable income for a married couple filing jointly; marginal capital gains income is taxed at half the marginal rates applicable to ordinary income below these levels. At higher taxable income levels the maximum capital gains rate cannot exceed 25 percent. The tax shelter factor falls gradually, reaching a low of about 0.28 for those in the highest taxable income brackets. At the margin, a is taken as 0.4 for individuals' capital gains. Nonlife insurance companies are treated as ordinary corporations with respect to capital gains; a for capital gains is 0.5. For individuals and nonlife insurance companies together, we assume a is 0.45.

We now have a $= 1$ (no shelter) for life insurance companies, pension funds, and the nonprofit sector (Group II) and for dividend income earned by nonlife insurance companies and individuals (Group III). a $= 0.45$ for capital gains income realized by Group III. Thus,

$$a_1 = 0.45\frac{0.01485}{0.04695} + \frac{0.03480}{0.04695}$$

$$= 0.88$$

We can now substitute into the equation and calculate the effect on the maximum average marginal tax rate applicable to after-removal interest income of the assumed shift, first for the minimum and then for the maximum increase in municipal yields:

$$\Delta t_a = 0.537(1 - 0.30)\left[0.07 - 0.58 - \frac{0.04695}{0.0477}(0.07 - 0.88 \times 0.58)\right]$$

$$= -0.041$$

$$\Delta t_a = 0.537(1 - 0.30)\left[0.07 - 0.58 - \frac{0.04695}{0.0558}(0.07 - 0.88 \times 0.58)\right]$$

$$= -0.053$$

In brief, the assumed shift in acquisitions would lower the actual average marginal tax rate applicable to after-removal state and local bond interest by at most 4 to 6 percentage points from the maximum (47.1 percent), or to a level of about 41-43 percent.[14]

If the shift is at all reasonable, it leads to the conclusion that the

[14] Actually, the average marginal tax rate may not fall to the 41-43 percent level, since the maximum (47.1 percent) used as a base to calculate the shift effect is too low. We showed earlier in this chapter that if all bond yields rise, as is to be expected, the maximum and minimums calculated here are understated. In addition, our present calculation of the shift effects rests on a crude estimate of r_e. We noted in footnote 4 that the average marginal tax rate applicable to after-removal state-local bond interest is not t_1 (47.1 percent) when the alternative investment has a higher after-removal yield, but instead is greater. Thus, if our estimate for r_e is too low, the maximum average marginal rate to use as a base would again be higher than 47.1 percent. However, recall that r_e includes only the realized portion of capital gains plus dividend income. If fewer capital gains are realized, r_e falls.

Moreover, there are "tax-sheltered" investments other than equities for individuals to turn to, some with "shelter factors" greater than in the case of equities. Indeed, the capital market participants spoke of real estate as well as equities as an alternative use of funds; one could also add investments in resources subject to depletion allowances and perhaps others.

What proportion of the shift by individuals might be into these other investments is obviously difficult to specify. Since such investments as real estate equity and oil equity are not readily marketable and bank-administered trust funds are unlikely to deal in these investments, it is unlikely that the majority of individuals would acquire these assets in lieu of municipals. On the other hand, we should not underrate the capacity of individuals to learn and accept ways of reducing their effective tax rates.

As an illustration, assume that the shift proportion accounted for by individuals in Group I is half to stocks and half to real estate equity, and that Group II supplies less mortgage money to real estate equity and buys more municipals to the extent that individuals supply more equity funds. Assume the shift otherwise is the same.

If the gross return on real estate equity investment were 15 percent per annum, and the tax shelter factor .15 (these seem reasonable from observing typical syndicate transactions), the maximum weighted average marginal tax rate would be lowered some 11 percentage points. This is considerably more than the previous case but would still leave the marginal tax rate above the maximum "breakeven" rate of 34.9 percent.

secondary shifting effects on the Treasury's revenue gain are not likely to amount to much; the earlier calculation of the maximum does not need to be modified very much. The reason for this is quite simple. Commercial banks have no tax shelters available, so they must make the same tax payments whether they continue to buy municipals or shift to the purchase of corporate bonds. The only offsets against the maximum rate arise from (a) the fact that the yield on equities relevant to the tax problem is estimated as being slightly below that on municipals, and (b) the existence of tax shelters for those to whom equities are shifted as a result of repeal of the tax exemption.

Comparison of Interest Saved and Revenue Lost

Since ranges for the increase in interest cost due to dropping the exemption were established, comparison with the revenue gain due to dropping the exemption will reflect the interest cost increase chosen. It is clear, however, that if the redistribution of purchases is anything like that conjectured here, the revenue gain will substantially exceed the interest cost increase. If the 30.7 percent minimum estimate of the rise in interest costs indicated earlier is used, an average marginal tax rate of 23.5 percent would be required for the revenue gain to equal the interest cost increase. The estimate of a reasonable average marginal tax rate of 41-43 percent is 1.74-1.83 times the 23.5 percent break-even rate. Using the maximum rise in interest costs (53.5 percent) implies a 34.9 percent "break-even" average marginal tax rate. The average marginal tax rate of 41-43 percent would be 1.17-1.23 times the "break-even" rate of 34.9 percent.

In summary, removing the exemption feature would almost certainly produce revenue to the federal treasury in excess of the interest cost increase to state and local governments.

State Taxation of Federal Interest

It is usually assumed that as a *quid pro quo* for eliminating the exemption the states and their political subdivisions would be

TABLE 20. Selected State Individual and Corporate Income Tax Rates, 37 States, July 1, 1960

State	Marginal Tax Rate for Individuals with $7,000 Net Income	Maximum Sur-Tax Rate for Corporations
Alabama..............................	5.0%	3.0%
Alaska...............................	4.2	9.4
Arizona..............................	4.0	5.0
Arkansas.............................	3.0	5.0
California............................	3.0	5.5
Connecticut..........................	—	3.8
Colorado.............................	6.0	5.0
Delaware.............................	7.0	5.0
Georgia..............................	4.0	4.0
Hawaii...............................	6.0	5.5
Idaho................................	9.5	9.5
Iowa.................................	3.8a	3.0
Kansas...............................	4.0	3.5
Kentucky.............................	5.0	7.0
Louisiana............................	2.0	4.0
Maryland.............................	3.0b	5.0
Massachusetts........................	7.4c	6.8
Minnesota............................	6.5	9.3
Mississippi...........................	3.0	6.0
Missouri..............................	3.0	2.0
Montana..............................	5.0	5.0
New Jersey...........................	—	1.8
New Hampshire.......................	4.3d	—
New Mexico...........................	1.0	2.0
New York.............................	5.0	5.5
North Carolina........................	6.0	6.0
North Dakota.........................	7.5	6.0
Oklahoma.............................	5.0	4.0
Oregon...............................	9.0	6.0
Pennsylvania.........................	—	6.0
Rhode Island.........................	—	6.0
South Carolina.......................	5.0	5.0
Tennessee............................	6.0e	3.8
Utah.................................	5.0	4.0
Vermont..............................	7.5	5.0
Virginia..............................	5.0	5.0
Wisconsin............................	4.0	7.0
District of Columbia...................	3.0	5.0

Source: Joint Economic Committee, *The Federal Revenue System, Fact and Problems,* 1961 (Government Printing Office, 1961), pp. 278–83.

a 3.75.
b Rate on 1st $500 investment income.
c 7.38.
d 4.25 on interest and dividends only.
e Interest and dividends.

granted the right to tax interest on federal obligations. The added revenue would partially compensate state and local governments for their higher interest costs. In addition, there might be some rise, though obviously slight, in federal interest costs. The revenue gain to the states and localities would not be general, however, for three reasons: (1) only states and localities with income taxes (personal or corporate) would benefit; (2) states and localities in which investors with large holdings of federal bonds reside would benefit disproportionately; and (3) in most states the power to levy income taxes is not granted to localities. The revenue accruing from taxing federal interest might not be disbursed by state governments to the localities facing financial problems because of higher interest costs.

How much of a revenue gain would the benefiting states get? A crude guess can be made from existing top state tax levels and the present distribution of federal interest among the states. Table 20 lists the states having personal income and/or corporate income taxes as of 1960, together with suggestive marginal rates. The rates for individuals apply to those with $7,000 income; corporate rates are the maximum surtax rates. Judging from the data in this table, a 5 percent marginal rate for individuals and a 7 percent rate for corporations receiving federal interest income seems reasonable.

The next questions are: What proportion of total federal interest is (a) received by the states having personal or corporate income taxes? (b) What portion of it is received by taxable individuals or corporations? The second part can be answered first. Of total federal interest payments, those to United States agencies and trust funds, Federal Reserve Banks, and state-local trust funds would surely not be subject to state taxes. In addition, most states have special tax formulas for insurance companies. Often premium income is used as the tax base; interest income generally would not be taxed. Finally, mutual savings banks, nonprofit organizations, and foreign holders would be wholly or partly exempt. Table 21 shows the effect of all these exclusions. Of $9.3 billion of gross interest paid in 1960, $5.2 billion or 56 percent would be received by those whose interest receipts would be subject to state taxes.

Next the proportion of the federal interest payments made to residents of states having income taxes must be ascertained. Data on the distribution of commercial bank receipts of federal interest by

TABLE 21. Estimated Interest on Federal Debt Subject to State Personal and/or Corporate Income Taxes, 1960

(*Billions of Dollars*)

Gross interest payments on federal debt............................		$9.3
LESS payments to		
U. S. Government agencies and trust funds........................	$1.5	
Federal Reserve Banks...	1.1	
Total..		2.6
Equals..		6.7
LESS payments to:		
State, local governments.......................................	0.6	
Foreign holders and nonprofit organizations.......................	0.4a	
Insurance companies...	0.3	
Mutual savings banks..	0.2	
Total		1.5
Equals *Federal interest payments subject to state taxes*................		5.2
Paid to:		
Individuals:		
Savings bonds...	$1.4	
Other..	0.8	
Commercial banks...	1.8	
Nonfinancial corporations......................................	0.8	
Miscellaneous investors..	0.3a	

Source: Treasury Department, Office of Debt Analysis.
a These are estimated on the basis of debt held by all "miscellaneous investors"—savings and loan associations, foreign holders, dealers, and nonprofit organizations.

states are available. For 1960, the 37 states having personal or corporate income taxes accounted for 65.4 percent of federal interest received by all insured commercial banks.[15] The holdings of federal debt by individuals at the end of 1960 were largely savings bonds. Treasury data on cumulative sales and redemptions of savings bonds by states were used to approximate the distribution of interest payments.[16] The 37 states with personal income taxes account for some

[15] Computed from data in *Annual Report of the Federal Deposit Insurance Corporation* (1960), pp. 166-74. The dollar figures are $1,171 and $1,790 million respectively.

[16] These data are unsatisfactory for determining savings bonds outstanding by states. Mainly, they are biased by migration. A purchaser may buy in Maine and redeem in Florida, and as a result both states' figures are made incorrect. Savings bonds are often used as travelers' checks. In addition the sales and redemption figures are not quite comparable—sales are for series E and H bonds and redemptions are for series A—E bonds. However, these are the only data available.

TABLE 22. Estimated Yield to States from Taxing Federal
Interest Payments in 1960

Recipients	Taxable Interest	Proportion in States Having Taxes	Assumed Average Marginal Tax Rate	Revenue Yield
Individuals..............	$2.2 billion	$0.9 billion	5%	$ 45 million
Banks, corporations, and others..............	3.0 billion	1.95 billion	7%	137 million
Total State Yield...				$182 million

40 percent of total savings bonds outstanding. We shall assume that this also indicates their share of interest receipts from federal securities. The remaining interest which would be subject to state income taxes is received by corporations and "others." This interest income was allocated between the two sets of states using the distribution of commercial bank interest income as a guide.

The approximate revenue yield had states been allowed to tax federal interest in 1960 is in the neighborhood of $180 million. Table 22 shows the calculation. This figure is at best suggestive of the approximate level which state revenues from taxing federal interest payments might reach.[17]

The granting of the reciprocal tax right to the states would presumably match the form of exemption repeal. If the exemption were removed only on new issues, it is likely that states could only tax interest on new issues of federal debt. The states would rapidly approach the limit of taxing interest on outstanding federal debt, however, because of the bunching of maturities on federal debt in the less than five-year range. Indeed, had the states been granted the right to tax interest on new federal debt at the beginning of 1960,

[17] It is overstated, because it is assumed that all of the $1.4 billion of interest received on savings bonds would be subject to state income taxes. As the Treasury has shown (see *President's Tax Message,* submitted by Secretary of the Treasury Dillion to House Committee on Ways and Means, May 3, 1961, p. 153), perhaps 70 percent of interest on savings bonds is unreported on federal income tax returns. There is no reason to expect better results if this were subjected to state income taxes. On the other hand, if a proposal for withholding on interest and dividends were put into effect by the federal government, a larger proportion of this income would probably be reported on state income tax returns.

at the end of that year they could have taxed federal interest on the applicable portion of some $78 billion of new issues.

All of the preceding does not account for future changes in the ownership of the federal debt and thus that part subject to state taxation. No allowance is made either for new states joining the roster of those having personal and corporate income taxes or for changes in rate levels by states already having such taxes. Further, no account is taken of the relative rates of growth of federal debt and state-local debt, which would affect the future advantage of reciprocal abolition gained by the two levels of government. It is unlikely that the states and localities would recoup their interest cost rise, especially if federal indebtedness does not rise greatly. If all state and local debt outstanding in 1960 had been issued without the exemption and with 30-50 percent higher interest payments, interest payments in 1960 might have been $600 million to $1 billion greater, in comparison with the $180 million yield to the states from taxing interest paid by the federal government.

CHAPTER VI

Outstanding State and Local Debt

ANY PROPOSAL to modify the federal tax exemption for state and local government securities must resolve the problems posed by the existence of more than $70 billion in outstanding bonds. Holders of presently tax-exempt issues will receive a windfall capital gain if interest payments received by holders of new issues are taxable and payments to holders of outstandings are not. Some of the inequity arising from tax-exemption will continue under these conditions until all of the tax-exempts mature—some forty or more years. Conversely, holders of presently outstanding bonds will suffer capital losses if tax exemption is eliminated for both new and presently outstanding issues.

In this chapter, first, some of the effects that are likely to occur and some revenue implications for the Treasury if interest from outstanding as well as new issues is made subject to tax are considered. Next some effects of taxing outstanding bonds are appraised. Specifically the effects on debt management, equity yields, and bank earnings are discussed. Finally, the revenue implications of a tax credit designed to equalize the tax applicable to new and outstanding bonds are explored.

Federal Revenue From Taxing
Outstanding Issues

Investors purchase bonds on the basis of after-tax yield. When income from a municipal bond is tax-exempt—and only the capital gain is taxable—bonds issued at substantial discounts from par will sell at a higher market yield than bonds selling at their par value. If the income from municipal bonds becomes taxable, the reverse becomes true; a deep discount bond will sell at a lower market yield than a bond whose coupon yield is equal to its market yield. As long as the tax laws encourage individual and corporate investors to prefer a dollar of income from capital gains to a dollar of ordinary income, market yields will reflect this preference.

A reasonable estimate of the effect of exemption removal on the yield (or price) of outstanding municipal bonds, similar to the one given in Chapters III and IV for new issues, is difficult to make. It will depend on the prevailing tax rates, expectations regarding possible changes in capital gains taxation, the proportion of municipal bonds now at a discount, and the maturity distribution of outstandings, among other things. But since many of the bonds are now at a discount, it is clear that preference for capital gains will lead to a smaller average increase in the market yield on outstandings than on new issues. This finding has implications for the direction of redistribution of outstanding securities as well as the revenue collected by the Treasury from a tax on outstanding issues.

Unless there is a change in the method of accounting for interest income, the Treasury would collect most of the personal and corporate income taxes on the interest paid at coupon rates, not market yields. Even though market yields on outstanding bonds would rise —assuming that the tax was applied to both new issues and outstandings—the Treasury would collect income taxes at the tax rates applicable to the old coupons. However, there would be important offsets if investors realize capital losses by selling their securities.

When the tax law is passed, an immediate effect of the legal change will be a fall in the market value of all outstanding municipal bonds.[1] This loss of market value is not negligible. Assume that the yield on outstandings averages 3.5 percent, that it rises on the average by 150 basis points to 5 percent (as suggested by the discussion in Chapter IV), and that the average maturity of the outstanding securities is ten years. Then approximately one-eighth of the value of outstanding securities would be eliminated.[2] This estimate must be treated as a crude approximation, since we do not know the average maturity of the outstanding municipals. We do know that the supply of new issues has increased rapidly in recent decades and that many serial issues place a major part of the offering in the more distant maturities, often at low coupon rates. But time has reduced the number of years remaining to maturity thereby lowering the average maturity of these issues. Further, the estimate assumes that the bonds are selling at par while the fact that yields have risen on new municipal issues over time suggests that most outstandings would sell below par if they were traded in the current market. The relative fall in market value will be the same for issues selling below par, but the absolute loss in dollars will be smaller for such issues. An alternative estimate, based on average maturity of seven and one-half years, will therefore be given in the footnotes.

A loss of one-eighth of the value of outstandings means that capital losses of roughly $9 billion[3] would be suffered by bondholders. It would clearly be advantageous for some holders who suffered the loss to sell their bonds, take the loss as a long-term capital loss for tax purposes, and invest either in an alternative security or (because of the prohibition on "wash sales") in another municipal issue. It is likely that commercial bankers would take advantage of this opportunity to the extent that they had taxable income since they are permitted to deduct capital losses from ordinary income in the computation of tax payments. Capital losses incurred by other

[1] Indeed, the contemplation of such a tax by the Congress would reduce the market value of the outstanding bonds if investors at the margin attach a moderate probability to eventual passage.

[2] If an average maturity of 7-1/2 years is assumed, the capital loss on outstanding securities is approximately 10 percent.

[3] Based on outstandings of about $72.3 billion as of the end of 1961. This reduces to about $7.3 billion if a 7-1/2 year average maturity is assumed

investors are not treated in this way. Therefore some of the effects of the applicable capital gains law will be described before the revenue yield to the Treasury is considered.

The present tax laws require that life insurance companies accrue any discount received at time of purchase. The discount is prorated over the life of the investment and taken as a supplement to ordinary income for tax purposes. Capital losses (long-term) can be charged against realized capital gains in excess of prorated discounts. It is unlikely that the life insurance companies would be able to establish sufficient capital gains to offset the losses on their portfolio of municipals implied by the taxation of municipal bond interest. Moreover, the tax treatment of deep discount bonds would encourage life insurance companies to prefer new issues to outstanding issues. This is so for the reason indicated below—the new issues would sell at a higher before tax yield than the outstanding issues. Thus, while taxation should increase the rate at which life insurance companies purchase municipal bonds, life companies will become a more important factor in the market for new issues as we have argued in Chapter V.

Individuals would suffer the largest losses since they are the largest holders. They would be allowed to deduct these losses from long-term and short-term capital gains in full and in addition would be allowed to deduct $1000 per annum of ordinary income before computing their tax. Their remaining losses could be carried forward and used in a similar manner for the following five years. Since there is no requirement that losses must be realized when they occur, individuals (and other groups) would be able to choose the date of realization so that they minimize their tax burden. Like banks, but to a lesser extent, it would pay individuals to realize some losses and reinvest in municipal bonds selling at deep discounts. In this way, they could defer a part of their tax payment to the future and lower the applicable tax rate.

The spread between the new issue yield and the yield on outstanding bonds in each quality class would adjust to reflect the preferences of buyers for capital gains. The marginal investor would be indifferent when faced with a choice between before tax yields. Banks, individuals subject to high marginal tax rates, and corporations would prefer to take their income as capital gains. Life insurance companies, mutual savings banks, and other tax sheltered investors would prefer to purchase new issues. As noted earlier, state and local pension funds would also become heavy buyers of new issues of state and local securities.

No doubt there would be a shift in the ownership of issues outstanding at the time that the tax is imposed. We have not estimated the final distribution, but it is likely that individuals, non-life insurance companies, and commercial banks will on balance be net sellers and that pension funds, life companies, and state and local governments will be net buyers. However, it is most unlikely that the distribution of presently outstanding bonds will resemble the new issue distribution. In addition to the preference for income in the form of capital gains, there is the problem of redistributing a large stock of securities through the capital markets. When these securities are widely scattered serial issues, redistribution becomes costly. In these circumstances, it seems reasonable to expect that those who wish to increase or reduce the size of their present portfolio of municipals will effect this adjustment principally by allowing new issues and retirements to adjust the stock over time.

The revenue yield to the Treasury from a tax on presently outstanding bonds will be $950 million in the first year, assuming that there is no shift in the distribution of outstanding debt at the time the tax is passed.[4] Assuming that there is some shift in the distribution of outstanding bonds, less than $950 million may be collected. Note however that while there may be substantial buying and selling, for reasons discussed above, it is the net redistribution which becomes important in the computation of the yield of a tax on presently outstanding bonds. That is, we must allow for both the revenue loss resulting from the shift of municipal bondholders into other tax shelters and the revenue gain arising from the shift out of

[4] Based on present interest payments in excess of $2 billion, the distribution of bonds among taxpayers and the average marginal tax rates shown in Table 14 above.

Of course, the effect of the redistribution of securities may raise the market yield on all debt (causing capital losses) and reduce the market yield on equities (causing capital gains). To evaluate this effect on the present value of tax collections, some assumptions about the amount and the time distribution of the realized gains and losses must be made. For simplicity, we have assumed that the revenue effects of the capital gains on equities balance the revenue effects from capital losses on debt. The reader may modify the subsequent estimates by the value that he assigns here.

tax shelters of the holders of securities which are sold in order to acquire municipal bonds.

In subsequent years, the amount of revenue received by the Treasury from a tax on municipal bond interest (1) will decline as the bonds outstanding on the date of exemption removal reach maturity, (2) will increase because capital gains must be realized when the bonds reach maturity, and (3) will be supplemented by the increasing gross revenue from the tax on new issues of state and local securities. The question of new issues was discussed in Chapter V. Here a rough estimate of the present value of the tax on the presently outstanding issues is provided. Before estimating the present value of the revenue gain, the loss in revenue resulting from the capital losses imposed on present bondholders is assessed.

Tax offsets will be substantial in the early years. For commercial banks there will be a tax credit equal to 52 percent of the loss of more than $2 billion, or about $1.2 billion.[5] Other holders, principally individuals, could deduct a smaller part of their losses. It seems reasonable to assume that neither commercial banks nor individuals would choose to realize all of their losses immediately. Instead, they would spread their losses over time, charging them against income in the case of commercial banks and against short-term and long-term capital gains in the case of individuals. Only a small part of the loss by individuals, $1000 per year per return, could be charged against ordinary income. However, by failing to realize all of their losses at the time they occur, individuals could increase the extent of deductibility beyond the six years allowed by the carry forward provision.

Assuming as a minimum that individuals offset their capital losses only against capital gains and that banks offset their losses at the 52 percent rate, the Treasury would lose more than $2 billion in taxes from these two groups.[6] And it is not unlikely that Congress

[5] If a 7-1/2 year average maturity is assumed, the capital loss would be about $1.8 billion and the tax credit would be $940 million. The capital loss for banks is assumed to be 25 percent of the total loss in each case—the proportion of outstanding municipals they hold times the loss.

[6] Specifically, about $2.2 billion, with banks accounting for $1.2 billion and individuals for $1 billion. Capital losses for individuals were estimated at about $4 billion, using the same procedure applied to banks. The tax loss from them was assumed to be 25 percent of this loss.

would add to the loss of net tax revenue by providing a credit for some of the losses inflicted on bondholders.

Capital values would be recovered as the bonds reached maturity. But the tax rate applicable to the gains would be the capital gains rate rather than the individual or corporate tax rates. These gains would be deferred for at least ten years on the average if the same assumption is maintained that was used in evaluating the amount lost. To assess the net gain or loss to the Treasury in the early years, the present value of the tax on these capital gains must be computed.

As an illustration of the most extreme case, assume that a commercial bank holds a $1000 tax-exempt selling at par and yielding 3.5 percent. Let the particular bond have ten years remaining to maturity. Let the bank sell this bond, take its loss and re-acquire a similar bond selling at $883, a price which will yield 5 percent on a 3.5 percent coupon held for ten years. To compute the tax revenue to the Treasury, three items must be added: (1) the present value of the tax (at 52 percent) on $35.00 received annually for ten years; (2) the present value of the tax on the capital gain of $117 received ten years hence; (3) the tax credit on a loss of $117 taken in the first year.

The algebraic sum of the present value of the tax receipts or offsets from these three items is approximately $105 using a 4 percent discount rate to equate present and future income to the Treasury. The present value of the tax receipts on the income from the bond (item 1 above) is nearly $150. The net effect of considering capital gains and losses is to eliminate almost one-third of the Treasury's receipts from the tax over the life of the bond in the particular case considered.[7]

Thus even in the most extreme case, where capital losses are deducted from ordinary income and are taken in the first year, the present value of the revenue gain to the Treasury from a tax on outstanding issues is positive. Clearly the present value of the tax on all outstanding bonds is positive. The following example illustrates

---

[7] In the first year of the tax, assuming that the capital loss is taken then, the revenue loss to the Treasury from imposing the tax is approximately $40.00. Using an average of 7-½ years to maturity, the total present value of the tax receipts is $74.75 and the revenue loss in the first year is approximately $30.00.

that this is true if the same general method of calculation is applied to the total stream of income from outstanding state and local securities.

Again assume that the average maturity is ten years. It is estimated above that if there are no shifts in the distribution of outstanding bonds, the Treasury will receive $950 million in the first year. Allowing for some shift in portfolios which on balance reduces the average marginal rate of the municipal bondholders, it is most unlikely that tax revenues would be less than $800 million in the first year.[8] As bonds mature, the amount of interest received will decrease. Because the receipts will be higher in the early years than in the later years, the present value of the tax paid on the interest is estimated at $4.5 to $5 billion over the life of the presently outstanding bonds. The present value of the tax on capital gains received in ten years adds $1.5 billion to the Treasury's revenue. Even if it is assumed that the tax offset for capital losses ($2.5 billion) is all taken in the first year, a most extreme assumption, the present value of the revenue gain from taxing outstandings is at least $3.5 to $4 billion over the life of the presently outstanding issues.[9]

Other Economic Effects

Debt Management Effects

An attempt to quantitatively appraise all of the shifts that would be set off by efforts to tax municipal bond income would go well beyond the scope of this study. In the end, any conclusions reached would be based largely on judgment and guess. Nevertheless, it is worthwhile considering some of the more likely shifts in a qualitative way, particularly because of the effect such shifting may have on Treasury debt management operations.

---

[8] It is clear that this is a minimum figure since it assumed an average marginal tax rate of 40 percent applicable to outstanding bonds after shifting—i.e., a lower tax rate than the rate computed in Chapter V.

[9] We have again used a 4 percent rate to equate present and future income to the Treasury. If Congress should elect to compensate the present holders of municipal bonds for the capital losses imposed or if capital loss offsets for tax purposes were liberalized, an additional offset against the revenue gain would result. The tax offset includes those for life insurance companies and "Other Insurance" companies, which would be about $200 million at most.

From earlier discussion with respect to shifting, it was concluded that individuals, commercial banks, and nonlife insurance companies would shift out of municipal bonds to some extent and that private pension funds, state and local pension funds, nonprofit organizations, and life insurance companies would shift into municipal bonds.

More attention will be directed to the market for long-term government bonds, defined as any government bond with ten or more years to maturity or first call. The patterns of shifting suggested above indicate that the imposition of the tax on municipal bonds will raise yields on long-term government bonds relative to other yields or produce a fall over time in the proportion of the debt with over ten years to maturity. For among those groups which are shifting into municipal bonds are some of the principal holders of long-term government bonds. Unless those groups shifting out of municipal bonds can be induced to hold a larger part of their portfolio in the form of governments, the net demand (at existing yields) for long-term governments would be smaller.

Data from the Treasury Survey of Ownership for February 28, 1962 support this conclusion. Commercial banks held more than 35 percent of net government debt[10] on that date. But their share of ownership of long-term debt was much lower—less than 4 percent of the total. Could they be expected to increase their holdings of long-term government bonds substantially? Doubtless some country banks would shift from municipals to governments if the tax were applied to the income from outstanding bonds. But the majority of banks would probably not purchase many additional long-term governments unless there were a substantial rise in interest rates. We shall return to this question shortly.

It was noted above that individuals would probably shift into equities. It is unlikely that a government bond would be regarded by them as a close substitute for the tax-exempt bonds no longer available.

Fire, casualty, and marine insurance companies are not large purchasers of federal government securities. The Treasury survey

[10] Net marketable government debt is defined as total interest bearing marketable securities net of (1) debt held by Federal Reserve Banks and U.S. Government investment accounts and (2) guaranteed issues.

shows that they hold about 2-3 percent of net long-term bonds. The tax on municipal bond income would alter the balance of their portfolios but not in the direction of more purchases of government bonds. Judging from their past practices, they too would become buyers of equities—presumably equities of high grade in their case.

Those who would switch into municipal bonds and out of Treasury bonds include large holders of Treasury securities. Detailed breakdowns for state and local pension funds and state and local general funds have recently been made available in the Treasury *Bulletin*. Approximately 75 percent of the pension funds and 60 percent of the general funds are now included in the Treasury survey. Dividing the reported figures by these percentages suggests that all state and local pension funds and general funds held respectively 29 percent and 13 percent of the net long-term government debt outstanding on February 28, 1962. If it is estimated that approximately 5 percent of the net long-term debt is held by private pension funds, almost 50 percent of the long-term governments were in the portfolio of these three groups at the end of February 1962.

State and local pension funds, private pension funds, and other tax-exempt institutions are generally willing to sacrifice some liquidity for yield. The principal reason goverment bonds are attractive to them at present is their higher market yield relative to other authorized investments. In many instances, laws and regulations restrict all or many of their purchases to governmental obligations —federal, state, or local. Taxation of income from municipal bonds would reverse the yield relationships, that is, municipals would have higher yields than governments, and would therefore become attractive to this group of investors.

Life insurance companies are also listed as one of the groups that would switch into municipal bonds. But they hold only a small share of the federal government debt, and their switch would come at the expense of corporate debt rather than government debt.

The preceding discussion suggests that there would be a larger desired shift out of long-term government bonds than into them. This should not imply that individuals, commercial banks, and others would not increase their holdings of long-term bonds. Doubt-

less they would be motivated by a desire to maintain some proportion of their portfolio in fixed income, relatively secure assets at
interest rates similar to those obtainable in recent years. But it is
unlikely that these groups would purchase additional quantities of
sufficient magnitude to replace the private and public pension funds
and general funds as customers for government securities. Either
yields on long-term government bonds would rise relative to other
yields or the proportion of the debt with more than ten years to
maturity would fall over time.

This point—and others in this section—are raised to indicate
the scope of some of the direct and indirect effects of introducing
taxation of outstanding state and local government securities. It
was earlier noted in detail that the failure to tax municipal bond
income in the past has had important consequences for the present
composition of investor portfolios. It has encouraged some investors
to prefer municipal to federal government bonds; others have been
induced to hold governments rather than municipals. In our judgment, taxing outstanding state and municipal bonds will on balance reduce the demand for federal bonds at existing yields.

Effect on Equity Yields

A shift into equities as a means of replacing the high bond yields
available on tax-exempts to individuals subject to high marginal
tax rates would raise the price and lower the yield on equities. This
would be particularly true for equities on which capital apprecia-
tion was expected to be large. Over time this would affect the yield
on all equities. Capital gains for holders of equities would offset,
at least in part, the capital losses suffered by bondholders.

As a result, corporations would issue less debt and more equity
since the cost of raising money through the sale of equity would
have fallen relative to the cost of selling bonds. Equilibrium would
be reached at a smaller spread between equity and bond yields and
a smaller proportion of new corporate financing in the form of bond
issues, thus promoting risk-taking and private investment. These
effects would be small, but they are a primary reason advanced by
most of those who favor removal of the tax exemption on state-local
government securities.

Effect on Bank Earnings

Commercial banks would suffer a sharp decline in earnings as a result of the tax on income from outstanding municipal bonds. Following Robinson's[11] method of calculating the interest income from municipal bonds, insured commercial banks earned more than $450 million in 1960 on their municipal portfolio. Total earnings after tax were $2 billion. At the 52 percent rate, the tax that would have been applicable to the income from municipals would have reduced their net after tax income by about 12 percent. No doubt this would necessitate substantial changes in the management of commercial bank portfolios.

The precise direction of the shift in commercial bank asset holdings is both difficult to forecast and beyond the scope of this study. One course would be to accept greater risk by granting loans at higher interest rates to borrowers who would be rejected under present standards. Probably they would add to their portfolio of long-term governments, as noted above, but this alone would not restore their income to former levels. Higher charges on checking accounts and other bank services would be another likely alternative. To the extent that tax-exemption subsidizes the users of bank facilities, an increase in service charges would reduce this subsidy.

Taxing Only New Issues

Taxing only the interest on new issues has been the usual form of exemption repeal proposals, with the notable exception of the Treasury proposal of 1942. Apparently this has reflected both the belief that taxing outstandings would be a breach of faith on the part of the federal government and the desire to avoid capital losses and the inequitable application of taxes to holders of existing securities.

Many of the effects which have been described above would occur if the tax is placed on new issues only. However, these effects would take place over time and would not require portfolio changes for outstanding issues of the magnitude described above. Other

[11] Roland I. Robinson, *The Postwar Market for State and Local Government Securities* (National Bureau of Economic Research, 1960), p. 85.

effects would be reversed, at least initially. Here the effect on outstanding issues of a tax on new issues, assuming that outstanding issues would not be taxed, is considered briefly.

Instead of capital losses, present holders would receive windfall capital gains. As the stock of tax-exempts diminished, that is, as old bonds reached maturity, those in the higher brackets would bid up the price of the outstanding bonds. Much of this effect would occur quickly since the available stock of tax-exempts will be fixed at the time the law is passed. The bonds would be transferred from income recipients in lower marginal tax brackets to those in higher brackets. The Treasury would of course realize a portion of the increase in value at the capital gains rate when the transfers were effected. Outstanding municipal bonds would sell at a premium. In this case, capital gains would precede capital losses (or amortization of premiums). The present value of the revenue stream would be positive.

Leaving the income from outstanding issues untaxed would perpetuate the inequity in the tax structure from this source until all outstandings mature. While this might be justified as necessary to avoid a breach of faith, windfall gains would be difficult to justify. This would amount to spawning further inequities through the tax laws.

It should be noted, however, that not all of the capital gains would be pure windfalls. The discounted value of the exemption feature would be included in the price received by holders of outstandings who elect to sell. Buyers of municipal bonds (with the exception of dealers) generally buy to hold to maturity. The receipt of capital gains would repay in a lump sum a percentage of the added income buyers planned to get in the form of tax-exempt interest. Only that part of the gain in excess of the present value of tax-exemption to the holder would be a true windfall. The size of the windfall would, of course, depend on the price that those in high marginal tax brackets would have to pay to induce those in lower income brackets to part with tax-exempt bonds.

Finally, it should be noted that the effects on debt management, bank income, and other economic effects similar to those described above would occur. However, in this case the force of such changes would be gradual and would have much less immediate impact on the capital markets.

Evaluation of a Tax Credit Proposal

An additional problem which would arise if both new and outstanding issues were taxed is the subject of an ingenious proposal by Lyle Fitch,[12] who showed that present holders of outstandings would be penalized if the same tax rate was applied to both new and outstanding issues. Holders of outstandings would continue to receive the interest payments agreed upon before the tax law was passed; holders of new issues would receive interest income at the yield structure applicable after the tax was imposed. Both would be taxed as if they had purchased fully taxable securities.

Fitch developed an elaborate scheme for computing a tax credit to deal with this problem. If calculated correctly, the credit would leave the holder of an outstanding bond with a net income equal to the net income he would have received had he purchased a taxable corporate bond at the time that he purchased his tax-exempt bond. The credit would be equal to the marginal tax rate times the assumed increase in yield which would have been paid on a taxable bond issued on the same date as the tax-exempt.

An example may make this clearer: Consider a bondholder in the 50 percent marginal bracket who owns a 5 percent municipal term bond maturing in 1970 which he purchased in 1949 for $1100. The relative differential for this grade bond and taxable corporate bonds in 1949 was 30 percent of the prevailing yield on municipals. The holder would have received a 30 percent higher yield had he bought a comparable taxable security in 1949. In 1960, he is paid $50.00 in interest, which is now taxable. His total annual income from the bond in 1960 would be $50.00 less $5.00 amortized premium, or $45.00. If he had bought the taxable corporate bond, his income in 1960 would have been $60.00 = $45.00 + $15.00 (= 0.30 × $50.00), and his tax liability is $30.00. When tax-exemption is eliminated, the tax due on his 1960 income is $22.50. Under the Fitch plan, he is allowed a $7.50 (= 0.50 × $15) credit against this tax, leaving

[12] Lyle C. Fitch, *Taxing Municipal Bond Income* (University of California Press, 1950), Chap. 7. A useful summary of this proposal is found in Vance N. Kirby, "State and Local Bond Interest," House Committee on Ways and Means, *Tax Revision Compendium*, Vol. 1 (1959), pp. 690-95.

him with a net income of $30.00, the same as if he had bought a corporate bond.

The plan has an obvious conceptual attraction. The bondholder would no longer enjoy excess benefits from exemption; at the same time, he would not be penalized for having bought exempt instead of taxable corporate bonds. As one observer put it, "This solution seems ideal; the inequity of undue tax savings is eliminated . . . and the actual investment made by the bondholder in the tax exemption feature of the bond is recognized."[13]

However, in practice, the problems involved in such a tax credit scheme would be substantial. In particular, it would be difficult to work up acceptable data for taxpayers to use for computation of the percentage increase in income assuming they had bought taxable instead of tax-exempt bonds.

Fitch envisaged the Treasury issuing tables for all dates of purchase, based on historical yield differentials. This would be very difficult. To calculate the relevant differential, new issue yields series would have to be computed for each grade of corporate bonds and tax-exempts at least monthly for something like the past thirty years. As was discussed in Chapter III, "the" average new issue yields on corporate bonds must consider private placement yields, and there is a paucity of long-run data on this subject. Moreover, long-term yields would not be sufficient since the municipal yield curve is more positively sloped than the comparable corporate curve. Purchasers who bought short or intermediate-term serials would naturally not accept as the alternative yields the long-term corporate new issues rate. In effect, a term structure of yields for past periods would be required (though the farther back one would go, the more the short-term yields could be ignored). It does not seem likely, in brief, that it would be possible to make yield calculations which would accurately reflect the investment in the exemption for all bondholders. Finally, it is arbitrary to assume corporate bonds as the alternative investment; as indicated in Chapter V, holders might have bought equities if the exemption had not been in effect.

In the second part of his scheme, Fitch sought to avoid the capi-

[13] *Ibid.,* p. 693.

tal losses which present holders would take in selling to others by applying the same tax credit scheme to future purchasers of outstandings. In this case the differential between taxable and tax-exempt yields used would be set permanently at the value prevailing at the time the exemption was dropped. In effect, the future buyer would obtain the benefit of exemption—indicated by the yield differential—in the form of a tax credit, but no more. The increase in after-tax yields on municipals to the level of corporate bond after-tax yields through the tax credit would prevent a fall in prices of outstanding municipals. There would still be capital gains and losses if corporate yields changed in the future, since after-tax yields on both would move together. However, these would have occurred had the exemption not been removed. This aspect of the Fitch scheme might be more workable. At least only one differential yield would be required instead of a series covering a long previous period.

CHAPTER VII

State Distribution of Tax Exemption Benefits and Alternative Subsidies

THE EXEMPTION for state-local government bond interest has been criticized not only on grounds of cost but also on grounds of efficiency. Critics have argued that the benefits of the tax exemption are poorly allocated because the size of the benefit increases directly with (a) the amount of borrowing and (b) the credit quality of the securities issued. The exemption is inefficient, it is argued, because neither borrowing nor credit ratings can be regarded as a suitable index of relative "need" of state and local governments for federal assistance. The details of these arguments were examined in Chapter II. This chapter provides quantitative evidence on the distribution of benefits and then discusses some alternative methods of subsidizing state and local governments.

Distribution of Benefits

Chart 5 compares, for forty-eight states, long-term state-local debt per capita and personal income per capita in 1957. The relation is not a close one (the Spearman rank correlation coefficient is 0.64), but clearly higher debt per capita is associated with higher

CHART 5. Per Capita State-Local Long-Term Debt and Per Capita Personal Income, By States, 1957

Per Capita Long-Term Debt

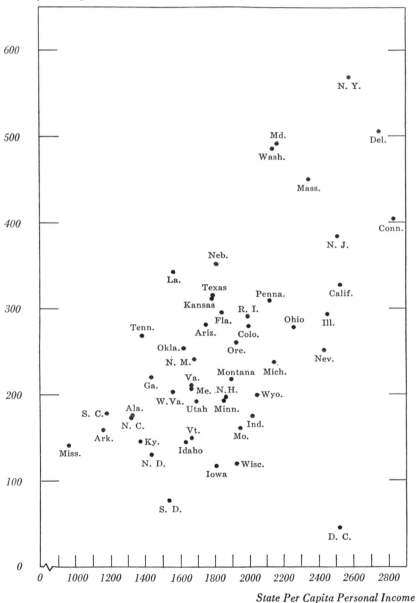

State Per Capita Personal Income

Source: U.S. Department of Commerce, *Statistical Abstract of the U.S.,* 1959, pp. 311 and 411.

104

personal income per capita. This bears out the contention that the subsidy involved in the exemption feature benefits governmental units in high-income areas more than those in low-income areas. If per capita income is taken as a measure of economic welfare, the exemption feature is an inefficient subsidy because it is tied to the amount borrowed and is not inversely related to income.

Robinson noted that the differential between municipals and taxable corporate bonds, stated as a percentage of corporate yields, was greatest for issues with the highest credit rating and least for the lowest credit rating securities.[1] On this basis, Maxwell concluded that the exemption was probably inefficient since governmental units with the lowest credit rating would probably be those most in need of subsidy and those with the highest credit rating would be least in need of subsidy.[2]

Chart 6 is designed to depict the extent to which there is an inverse relationship between credit rating and need. It compares, for the year 1957, an index of the quality of state-local bond issues in each state with personal income per capita. The index of credit quality is based on the proportion of gross issues in each Moody's credit category as computed by the IBA. Values (from 1 to 5) are assigned to each category. The highest rating (Aaa) is scored 5, Aa is rated 4, etc. For each state, these were multiplied by the percentage of gross issues in each category.[3] Although the data in Chart 6 are by no means conclusive, they do suggest that average credit ratings for the communities in the various states issuing securities in 1957 bore little relationship to average state per capita incomes. (The Spearman coefficient is .19.)

More important to the economic welfare argument is the changed relationship during recent years in the yield differential between municipals and corporate bonds in the different quality classes. As shown in Chart 1, the difference in relative differentials for Aaa and Baa securities, measured by yields on outstanding issues, has narrowed since 1956: by 1960, the relative spreads were

---

[1] Roland I. Robinson, *The Postwar Market for State and Local Government Securities* (National Bureau of Economic Research, 1960).

[2] James A. Maxwell, "Exclusion from Income of Interest on State and Local Government Obligations," House Committee on Ways and Means, *Tax Revision Compendium*, Vol. 1 (1959), p. 715.

[3] The basic data were furnished by the Investment Bankers' Association.

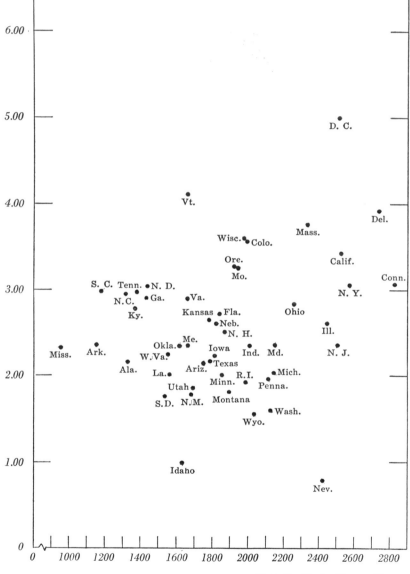

Credit Quality Index

State Per Capita Personal Income

Source: Investment Bankers' Association and U.S. Department of Commerce, *Statistical Abstract of the U.S.,* 1959, p. 411.

virtually the same for both rating classes. Morris has noted that the ratio of Baa to Aaa new issues yields on municipals has shown a fairly steady downward trend since 1956.[4] It appears that investors have become aware that the yield differential between low- and high-quality municipals was not justified by higher default and final loss experience on the low-quality issues. As a result, investors aggressively entered the low-quality segment of the market and changed the credit quality yield structure. This parallels experience in the corporate bond market earlier in the postwar period.

Since there is apparently no relationship between credit rating and income, and since the difference in interest costs between high and low quality municipal issues has been narrowing, it cannot be assumed that the tax exemption subsidy discriminates between communities with different ratings.[5] On the other hand, it seems clear from the data that the subsidy from the tax exemption is not distributed in a way which will tend to equalize per capita income among the states.

Alternative Subsidies

Suggestions for abolishing the exemption feature have usually been coupled with proposals to provide alternative federal subsidies as compensation. Not to do so would make repeal politically impossible. Moreover, it is generally accepted by opponents of the exemption feature that some undesirable curtailment of investment in social capital might otherwise result from higher interest costs. The proposed subsidies would be an addition to the increased revenue states would receive from taxing interest on federal obligations.

Two forms of subsidy will be discussed. One type of subsidy may be considered a quid pro quo for the states and their localities surrendering the benefits of the exemption feature. A subsidy of this kind might be tied to state and local borrowing in one of several ways. Another kind of subsidy might be tied to capital outlays rather than borrowing. In this case the subsidy would not be strictly allocated according to exemption benefits lost.

[4] Frank E. Morris, "An Examination of Yield Indexes on Municipal Bonds," *IBA Statistical Bulletin* (September 1960).

[5] This is also Morris' interpretation. See *ibid.*, p. 4.

Regardless of the form of subsidy used, the degree of federal control and supervision over its use is bound to be a major issue. With the exemption feature, benefits are set and distributed by market forces, albeit somewhat haphazardly and inefficiently. An alternative federal subsidy may not be as free of federal control. Most observers support the usual purposes to which the exemption benefit is put by local governments. Those who view with alarm the potential federal intrusion into state-local affairs place great weight on federal "interference" as an argument for the exemption and against alternative federal subsidies; those who minimize this possibility, or who favor greater federal intrusion, will support some alternative form of subsidy as against the present exemption feature. This study will not seek to resolve this difference by assessing the degree of federal control which may result from each possible alternative subsidy. For this reason, the political aspects are omitted in the following brief review of the various subsidy proposals.[6]

Subsidies for Borrowing

THE SELTZER PLAN. In 1941 Lawrence Seltzer proposed a simple way of compensating the states and their political subdivisions for loss of the exemption benefit—the federal government could pay some fixed proportion of their annual interest payments.[7] He proposed paying about 15 percent of their interest costs, a figure he felt would have been a bit greater than the rise in interest costs at that time. He suggested that the excess would encourage rapid re-

---

[6] There may be some question whether there should be any subsidy at all—exemption feature or otherwise. It could be argued that a good deal of the need for subsidization stems from inefficiencies due to irrational size and organization of local governments. As long as local governments can benefit from lower interest costs or some alternative subsidy, there may be too little pressure to rationalize, not only financing, but other aspects of the everyday business that local governments engage in. If some consolidation of local government jurisdictions is justified, the excessive costs per unit of "output" might be dramatized by loss of the exemption feature with no subsidy to replace it. In brief, do we want 100,000 local government units? Could many of the financing problems be solved with a bit of centralization at this level? This question is, of course, much more basic than the question of which subsidy might replace the exemption feature, and it is surely a problem which future research should explore fully.

[7] National Tax Association, *Proceedings* (1941), p. 195.

tirement of outstanding debt in lieu of taxing interest payments on it.

The plan has several advantages. First, it would eliminate the inequity of the exemption yet preserve the borrowing advantage of the states and localities. Second, it would be simple, definite, and fairly easy to administer. Third, being proportional to interest payments, it approximates the maintenance of the differential advantages of the exemption feature to different borrowing units.

The figure of 15 percent need not, of course, be rigid. Indeed, the portion of after-removal interest payments which currently would represent higher interest costs would more nearly be in the 23-35 percent range, as was noted in Chapter III. The figure would depend on the existing relative yield differential, and, obviously, on how little the states and localities would be willing to accept.

THE FITCH TAX CREDIT PROPOSAL. Fitch suggested that his plan for a tax credit to future purchasers of outstandings be used to maintain the borrowing differential to the states and localities. (See Chapter VI.) It will be recalled that the plan provides a tax credit that in principle equalizes the after tax yield on corporate and taxable municipal bonds. This would allow municipals to sell at lower before tax yields than corporates without inequity among taxpayers. Essentially the same plan was suggested in a recent CED policy statement.[8] Like the Seltzer plan this type of alternative would be definite. In addition, it would give the illusion of a subsidy established by market forces, though "the" actual differential would be written into the tax credit provision by legislation. Its main fault is that it would be difficult to administer, as noted earlier. In practice it would probably be much easier to maintain the borrowing advantage of local governments through some version of the Seltzer plan.

DISTRIBUTING TO STATES AND LOCALITIES REVENUES FROM TAXING FUTURE ISSUES. The Treasury Department Committee on Intergov-

[8] Committee for Economic Development, *Growth and Taxes: Steps for 1961* (1961), pp. 14-17.

ernmental Fiscal Relations[9] suggested, in 1943, that the Treasury redistribute to the states the revenue from taxing new issues of state and local government securities. The redistribution would be proportional to the annual interest payments on fully taxable issues made by each borrowing authority.[10] The major weakness in such a proposal is that it might involve compensation more than, equal to, or less than the rise in interest costs to particular states and localities. Its main advantages are definiteness and simplicity. It would involve the Treasury in accounting for the revenue gained from taxing state-local interest, but the usual tax forms could easily be adjusted to this purpose.[11] An additional disadvantage, however, might be that the subsidy would vary every time federal tax rates changed.

SPECIAL INTERMEDIARY ASSISTANCE. One way of subsidizing state and local government borrowing would be through a special federal or semiofficial intermediary which could lend at low rates. Such an institution could be large and empowered to borrow specified amounts with the full guarantee of the federal government; it could be conceived on a smaller scale with no borrowing power of its own but with a revolving fund; or it could be some variant in between. Hansen and Perloff[12] proposed an "Intergovernmental Loan Corporation" which "should be authorized to purchase the securities of state and local governments at a rate of interest which would reflect the cost of borrowing to the federal government plus a carrying charge (including in the computation of the charge probable losses through defaults)."[13] This would be a revolving fund type lending institution, with no restriction on the proposed use of proceeds or other eligibility requirement.

[9] Treasury Committee on Intergovernmental Fiscal Relations, *Federal, State, and Local Government Fiscal Relations*, S. Doc. 69, 78 Cong. 1 sess. (Government Printing Office, 1943).

[10] Redistribution on the basis of debt outstanding rather than interest charges would give disproportionate advantages to issues of short-term or high-grade securities over issues of long-term or low-grade securities.

[11] See Lyle C. Fitch, *Taxing Municipal Bond Income* (University of California, 1950), p. 118.

[12] Alvin H. Hansen and Harvey Perloff, *State and Local Finance in the National Economy* (W. W. Norton & Co., 1944), pp. 203-05.

[13] *Ibid.*, p. 204.

TABLE 23. Federal Aid to State and Local Governments,
By Major Activity, 1960

(*Millions of Dollars*)

Activity	Federal Aid[a]
Highway construction...	$2,942
Public assistance..	2,059
School lunch, surplus commodities, and other agriculture......................	507
Housing and urban renewal...	377
Education and science..	365
Unemployment compensation and employment service.......................	319
Health, natural resources, and other.....................................	605
Total...	$7,174

Source: Bureau of the Budget, *Special Analysis of Federal Aid to State and Local Governments in the 1962 Budget*, p. 3.
[a] Includes budget and trust funds.

One variation in the federal lending agency idea would be an institution with relatively modest resources designed to support issues of small, unrated borrowing units. It is by no means certain that such issues could not be sold without special assistance if the exemption feature is removed. However, such support might be the solution to this particular problem, should it develop.

Proposals to establish government intermediaries have been criticized because they add to the already lengthy list of special federal lending agencies. Furthermore, subsidies in this form are less obvious and definite, and hence often more easy to "sell," whereas for public evaluation and intelligent appraisal, future subsidies might well be made open and straightforward.

Subsidies for Capital Outlays

One criticism of the exemption feature, discussed in Chapter II, is that it subsidizes only capital formation financed through borrowing. Capital formation financed out of current state-local receipts is neither aided nor encouraged by tax-exemption. The argument is made that the subsidy is inefficient. Areas most in need of facilities often are not inclined to borrow.

Proponents argue that if the only question were which subsidy would satisfy more pressing "needs" per dollar spent, a subsidy tied to capital outlays and inversely related to community wealth and income would be most desirable.[14] In fact, a number of programs already in effect operate in part on this principle. In 1960, state and local governments received some $7.2 billion of federal assistance. As Table 23 shows, much of this aid is of a sort which directly supports state-local capital outlays. This is certainly true of the grants for "highway construction," "housing and urban renewal," and to some extent for outlays for "health, natural resources and other" and "education and science." Federal aid to state-local capital outlays in 1960 probably totaled some $4.3 billion. In most cases, however, the aid is not tied to any index of state-local wealth or income. Several proposed programs would incorporate this feature in one way or another; the new "depressed areas" legislation and the proposed federal aid to schools programs would give priority to capital outlays of poorer regions or states.

In short, there is nothing new in federal aid for those state-local outlays deemed to be of national importance. They are already sizable and have a long history. This form of alternative subsidy merits consideration along with subsidies tied to state-local borrowing.

[14] Implicit in this is some assumption of the desirability of "balanced growth"—whereby subsidies should be allocated to improving conditions in lagging regions and communities so that all will grow together. However, it is not at all established that the aggregate growth rate would be higher under this approach than where subsidies are used to lend additional impetus to leading sectors and regions.

CHAPTER VIII

Summary of Discussion at the Experts' Conference

THE CONFERENCE DISCUSSION centered on a selected, but important, set of issues relating to the tax treatment of interest income from state and local government securities: (1) the value of the federal tax exemption, in terms of lower interest costs, to state-local governments; (2) the market for state-local bonds if the exemption feature is removed; (3) the revenue implications of the present treatment; (4) effects of exemption removal on Treasury debt management; and (5) the political aspects of the present tax treatment and of alternative methods of reducing state-local borrowing costs.

The conference was not intended to come to conclusions regarding the merits of the present tax provisions applying to state and local government bonds. Its primary purpose was to discuss and attempt to evaluate the economic effects of the present treatment or changes in it, with particular emphasis on the effect of the exemption (or its removal) on state-local borrowing costs and on federal revenues. Many of the participants felt that these issues cannot be discussed adequately without bringing in the political consequences of changing the present law, and about one quarter of the time was spent on that aspect of the subject. However, the participants agreed—some reluctantly—to the chairman's ruling that the

conference would not discuss the constitutional issue. This ruling
was considered necessary because the background materials, which
were prepared by economists, did not discuss this issue and few
participants were attorneys by profession.

As it developed, the discussion was confined to the effects of
removing the exemption from new issues only. With few dissents,
it was agreed that taxation of interest on outstanding issues would
raise difficult practical problems and that the Congress would, in
any event, regard such a step as an unwarranted violation of a past
commitment.

"The" Yield Differential

Perhaps the most important practical question raised in any discussion of policy on this subject is the value of the tax exemption,
in terms of reduced borrowing cost, to the units of government doing the borrowing, that is, the interest rate differential between taxable and tax-exempt securities of comparable quality. Most of those
who defend tax exemption say that the differential is large—in
other words, that state-local borrowing costs would rise substantially if the exemption were removed. Those who oppose the exemption by and large agree that state-local borrowing costs would
rise, but most of them feel that proponents of the exemption overstate the increase by a considerable margin.

The background paper presented statistical evidence regarding
the differential, summarized the opinions of several knowledgable
capital market experts, and then calculated an estimated range on
the basis of the available data for private placements and public issues of corporate bonds (see Chapter III). The conference discussion of these points demonstrated how difficult it is to draw quantitative conclusions on this question from the information now
available. Nevertheless, a sense of the probable range of estimates—
admittedly broad—became evident as the discussion proceeded.

The evidence in the background paper on the relationship between corporate and municipal bond yields consisted of (1) a comparison of corporate and municipal bond yields in the period 1900-
13, when neither type of interest was taxed; (2) a comparison of Canadian municipal and corporate bond yields for recent years (Can-

ada taxes income from both sources); and (3) yields on bond issues of religious institutions in the United States which are similar in many respects to the bond issues of the smaller units of government in this country. The first two items of information suggested that yields on municipal bonds, if they were made taxable, would not exceed the yields on corporate bonds of comparable quality; the third suggested that even small municipal issues could be sold at a 5½ percent to 6 percent interest cost (at least, under the conditions prevailing in 1960).

A number of the participants felt that this evidence was not conclusive. First, they questioned the relevance and accuracy of the 1900-13 data to the current situation. Second, the published data for Canada were not regarded as reliable indicators, because local government units in Canada apparently raise a substantial proportion of their capital funds by issuing bonds directly to provincial governments or their agencies. Third, it was alleged that the yields of religious bond issues cannot be used as a basis of comparison, because the demand for such bonds is strongly affected by religious affiliation. On the other hand, it was pointed out that the 5½-6 percent range of the religious bond yields for 1960 was in the neighborhood of mortgage yields in that year. Several participants commented that there is no evidence that municipalities would be required to pay higher interest rates than home owners do.

The method used in the background paper to estimate the yield differential was discussed at length. It was noted that the "self-rating" of private placements by insurance companies probably overrated the quality of these issues relative to the ratings which would be given by private rating services. There are also difficulties in making comparisons between general yield indexes for corporates and municipals, because corporate issues have a wide variety of "fringe features" which municipal issues do not ordinarily have, for example, convertibility, warrants, and call features.

Banks and insurance companies apparently view as very important such collateral fringe benefits gained from holding corporate bonds as deposit balances, group insurance policy sales, trusteeships from corporations, and pension fund relationships. In short, it was felt that a comparison of corporate and municipal bond yields must make a correction for as many of these differential features as possible. Some stated that the yield differential can be calculated only on the basis of an issue-by-issue comparison of municipals and corporates, and only after a quantitative allowance has been made for the various fringe features. It was noted in this connection that, although specific sales within a day or so of the start of the conference indicated a long-term differential within the range estimated in the background paper (for example, a 150 basis-point interest differential between bonds issued by New York State and those issued by the World Bank), this can vary significantly over time and with the quality level and other features of the bonds involved.

A basic problem in measuring the probable rise in interest costs resulting from exemption removal is the effect such removal would have on the term structure of offering yields on municipals. The original background paper assumed that offering yields of all maturities would rise by the same absolute (basis points) amount as the estimated rise in offering yields of long-term issues. Several participants expressed the view—based on their appraisal of short-term yield relationships—that this understated the differential, on the ground that medium- and short-term rates would rise by a greater absolute amount than that indicated for long-term issues. In support of this opinion, the "flat" characteristics of the yield structure on religious bonds was cited.

Several suggestions for estimating the after-removal yield structure for municipals were made. One possible starting point is the yield curve on United States Treasury obligations, but some conferees noted that the curve might be affected by Federal Reserve open market operations and Treasury refunding policies; the middle range especially may be distorted by the existence of discount notes or bonds. In reply, it was observed that monetary and debt management policies are quickly reflected in corporate and municipal yields as well, and that the objection is relevant only for short periods. Some suggested that a larger and more representative sample of religious bond issues would be helpful, and others proposed the use of serial issues of Canadian municipalities.

The consensus seemed to be that state and local governments would not significantly change the maturity pattern of their bond issues in response to the change in the yield structure. In particular, the participants agreed that municipalities would not increase their use of term issues; the feeling was strong that few issuers would even consider returning to term issues and the sinking fund problems that accompanied them before serial issues became common.

A matter of great importance to the question of exemption removal is, of course, the trend in the yield differential. If the value of the exemption feature to the states and localities is likely to decline, municipalities might be more receptive to an alternative arrangement. There was some disagreement, however, regarding both recent changes in the differential and its future course. Some expected the growing needs of the states and localities to continue to raise the amount of state and local debt relative to other fixed interest bearing debt and to narrow the yield differentials between taxable securities and municipals.

Others did not agree. They granted that the differential is definitely lower now in relation to market yields than it was immediately after the war, but argued that it has not changed substantially since 1953. It was noted that in 1946 the market for municipals was too abnormal to provide a base for calculating the trend in the relative differential; the supply of tax-exempts was small then, and the differential was not of much value to the states and localities since they were not borrowing in significant amounts. Further, the absolute differential was about the same then as it is today, and the interest cost saving depends on the absolute, not the relative differential. Beyond this, structural changes on the demand side might offset any supply effects. For example, the recent change in Federal Reserve Regulation Q (which permitted commercial banks to increase their interest rates) might offset any tendency for the differential to narrow. Further, it was pointed out that the future trend of the differential would depend in no small measure on the general state of the capital markets in years ahead. Since state-local bond issues are somewhat responsive to market rates of interest, generally high levels of private capital outlays might reduce the supply of new state-local offerings in a given year.

To sum up this part of the discussion, the participants were asked to submit their judgments (in a closed ballot) of the possible range of increase in long-term municipal bond yields if the exemption were removed on new issues as of the time of the conference.

The judgment was to be based on a 15-20 year serial of a "readily marketable" issue, which was not a "deep discount" bond, following a period of market readjustment to removal of the exemption. The results, in basis points, were as follows:

Measure	Minimum Differential	Midpoint of Ranges	Maximum Differential
Range................	75–260	100–270	125–280
Median...............	125	150	200

The estimates of the minimum long-term yield differential varied from 75 to 260 points, while the estimates of the maximum differential varied from 125 to 280 points. The medians of the minima and maxima gave a much narrower range of 125-200 points, which was almost identical with the range estimated in the background paper. The median midpoint of all the ranges given was 150 points. Although the results of the informal poll suggest that there remains a significant difference of opinion on this point, the range of the median estimates is probably a good measure of the area of agreement among experts with divergent backgrounds and interest. In fact, the median midpoint of 150 basis points was mentioned several times in the later discussion as a working approximation of the value of the differential.

Markets for Taxable Municipals

The basic problem in estimating the revenue consequences of removing the exemption feature is to determine who would purchase a taxable municipal bond and what alternative outlets present holders of municipals might seek. The background paper started with the present distribution of holdings of corporate securities as a guide to determining which investor groups would buy taxable municipals, since these securities would presumably yield at least as much as corporates. However, this distribution was adjusted to increase the proportion of municipal purchases assigned to state-local trust funds and commercial banks and to reduce the proportions assigned to life insurance companies. The final distribution assumed that, while individuals, commercial banks, and nonlife insurance companies would reduce their purchases of municipals substantially, life insurance companies, state-local trust funds, pension funds, and other nonprofit institutions would take up the slack. As noted previously, the discussion of this as well as other points assumed that the removal of the exemption would apply only to new issues of state and local government securities.

In general, the participants agreed with the direction of the assumed shifts, but some questioned the magnitudes. For example, there seemed to be no disagreement that commercial banks would reduce their purchases of municipals if they were made taxable. Several interesting points were made, however, bearing on the magnitude of the shift and the alternative investments to which banks might turn. Taxable municipals might be regarded by banks as substitutes for term loans rather than for corporate bonds; if this were the case, the share of corporate bonds now held by the banking system would understate their potential interest in taxable municipals. On the other hand, the collateral business relationships arising from holding corporate bonds would give banks strong incentives to shift to these if municipals were made taxable. Depending on yields, banks might even shift partly from municipals into United States government securities. It was also pointed out that very large banks and the mass of smaller banks would probably react differently—the former would shift out of municipals almost completely, but the latter group would probably continue to hold them. Moreover, to some extent banks are obliged to hold municipals as collateral for public funds. Bank holdings of municipals do in fact parallel holdings of public (state and local) deposits. This practice might reduce the magnitude of the shift of commercial bank assets out of municipals, particularly for banks outside of New York City.

The investment practices of state-local trust funds in a capital market having taxable municipals evoked considerable interest. There was no question that these funds would have strong incentives to shift into municipals at the higher yields, as evidenced by the fact that they have shifted, in recent years, to higher-yielding corporate bonds in place of lower-yielding United States government securities. However, some participants felt that any shift into municipals offering yields comparable to corporates would be relatively minor, mainly because more and more public trust funds were being authorized to purchase equities. This will probably continue to be the future direction of their investments. It was suggested that the rise in yields and interest costs might induce the funds to buy municipals at "pegged" rates lower than market rates, but this was regarded as most unlikely because fund managers are primarily interested in earnings and view this as a major aspect of their trustee obligations. Several participants questioned how far the tendency to shift to equities would go on the grounds that current expectations of higher price levels may be reversed, that fund managers were familiar with bonds but not with equity investment, and that the rise in yields on fixed-interest bearing securities as yields on equities declined would eventually halt the shift to equities. All agreed that, at some yield on corporates and municipals (figures of 5-6 percent were mentioned), state-local trust funds would probably prefer these securities to equities.

In the case of individuals as an investor group, some of the participants thought the shift assumed in the background paper—from municipals to equities—was exaggerated; others disagreed. The first group felt that the popularity of equities in recent years is unusual and cannot be projected indefinitely into the future. In their view, it reflects past expectations concerning inflation and may in part be a "stock" adjustment of individuals' portfolios to a higher ratio of equity to debt securities. Once this ratio was attained, a larger percentage of new saving (or new funds) would be invested in bonds in order to maintain the newly established equity-debt ratio. Further, at some point, rising yields on fixed interest-bearing securities and falling yields (capital gains plus dividends) on equities would reduce the flow adjustment of individuals toward equities. Finally, changes in "fashion" or taste for equities (and possibly changes in the taxation of capital gains) might reduce the magnitude of the shift.

In contrast, the group which felt that the shift in individual portfolios from municipals to equities would be substantial stated that municipals are sufficiently "different" to require special attention and analysis, and are worthwhile now only because of the high after-tax return due to the exemption feature. On the basis of their knowledge of the attitudes of investors, several stated flatly that personal trust fund managers and high income individuals would not consider municipals if it were not for the tax advantage. Since a large part of individuals' holdings of municipals are under trust fund management, the managers of these funds would doubtless play a crucial role in the ultimate reception given to taxable municipals.

The discussion of the reaction of nonlife insurance companies to removal of the tax exemption for municipals was brief. These companies, it was agreed, would substantially reduce their purchases of municipals and shift largely into preferred stock.

In contrast, it was the consensus that life insurance companies would invest much more heavily in municipals than they do now. One influence on the magnitude of the shift would be the outcome of the current discussions with the Treasury of the tax treatment of life insurance company income from municipals. If a new interpretation were forthcoming, it would increase somewhat the present incentive of life insurance companies to hold exempt municipals. In these circumstances, there would be a smaller shift into taxable municipals than the shift assumed in the background paper. It was agreed that life insurance participation in the market for taxable municipals would largely be in the "long" end of the serial issues. But small life insurance companies might not shift as much as the large companies, because of problems of portfolio diversification, liquidity, and transactions costs.

Opinion diverged about the quality of the issues which life companies would buy. Some noted that life insurance companies apply more rigorous credit standards than most major investor groups; their entrance into the municipals market with substantial funds might, as a result, widen the spread between yields on low- and high-rated municipals. Others pointed out that many life insurance companies now buy the lower quality, higher yielding issues. There was considerable discussion of the potential attractiveness to life insurance companies of small and medium-sized issues of municipals if they were to become taxable. Some felt that the difficulties of analyzing the credit worthiness of the many small governmental units might restrict the investment of life insurance companies to large, national issues. Others disagreed, citing the mass credit analysis currently applied to mortgages by the life insurance companies.

In summary, the discussion indicated that in general the group agreed with the judgments made in the background paper with regard to the market for municipals in the event they were made taxable, although there were some differences of opinion on details. It seems fairly clear that, if the exemption feature were removed, state-local trust funds, life insurance companies, and nonprofit institutions would move aggressively into municipals, while commercial banks, nonlife insurance companies, and high-income individuals would probably move out of municipals into other types of investments.

Federal Revenue Gain

On the basis of the investor reactions and the yields of alternative investments assumed in the background paper, the conclusion that the revenue gain to the Treasury would substantially exceed the interest cost increase to the states and localities followed inevitably from the algebra. Nevertheless, several participants stated that in the time they had available to study the background paper they had not been able to follow the algebraic analysis closely. They expressed the view that since the values assumed for the variables could not be estimated with precision, it is doubtful that the problem was susceptible to such treatment.

It was further noted that several factors would modify the calculations and should be further investigated: (1) no account was taken in the calculation of a possible general rise in interest rates—but the conferees were not in agreement that there would be such a rise; (2) equity investments other than corporate stock might be considered as alternative investments by high-income taxpayers, especially real estate purchases; (3) United States government bonds that are acceptable at par in payment of estate taxes might become more attractive, and this would create nontaxable capital gains rather than taxable income for the purchaser; (4) the capital gains return in the calculation was based on an abnormal bull-market period; (5) the interest cost differential for municipals with and without the exemption may be larger than the ranges used in the computations; and (6) reciprocal state taxation of federal securities may increase the interest costs of the federal government. The net effect of all of these factors on the revenue estimate was discussed, but no agreement was reached.

Finally, it was pointed out that any alternative compensation to the states and localities would have to provide a considerable financial margin in their favor. To be sure that no municipality was hurt, the aggregate subsidy to all municipalities might exceed the revenue to be gained by the Treasury. This was by no means a general view—it was held only by those who favored the retention of the present exemption.

Treasury Debt Management

The effect of removing the exemption feature on federal debt management problems presented another contrast in views.

One view was that, if municipals were made taxable, the Treasury would find it more difficult to market its debt, that is, the Treasury would be able to market its securities only at somewhat higher yields. The magnitude of additional interest cost suggested was of the order of one-quarter of a percentage point. Those taking this position did so on the ground that some present purchasers of long-term governments (those subject to low taxes and, specifically, state and local pension funds were mentioned) would shift from governments to municipals at the higher yields, and those shifting out of municipals would not shift to governments and take up the slack.

The other view was based on the commonly stated thesis that Treasury securities are more difficult to market because municipals are tax exempt. According to this view, removal of the exemption on municipals might make Treasury obligations more attractive and lower their yields. It was also pointed out that the problems of federal debt management cannot be discussed without taking overall monetary policy into account. Presumably, changes in the level of interest rates could be offset by action of the monetary authorities.

It was noted that the effects on debt management could not readily be discussed without considering the revenue gain to the Treasury of removing the exemption feature and possible alternative federal compensation to the states and localities. If the states and localities were compensated no more than for the loss of the value of the tax exemption, net federal revenues would rise. This could mean a reduction in the rate of growth (or an increase in the rate of decline) of federal indebtedness—thereby slightly lessening Treasury debt management problems.

Political Aspects

The session of the conference devoted to the political aspects of the policy of tax exemption for municipals produced the most spirited exchanges and the widest divergence in opinions. Much of the discussion centered on the extent to which substitution of an alternative form of compensation to the state and local governments for the tax exemption on their securities would increase federal control over state-local fiscal affairs.

A significant difference that soon became apparent involved the definition of the term "increase in federal control." The basic problem here was the difference in interpretation of the origins of the present exemption feature. Some participants argued that the present exemption had only a legislative foundation and could be altered if Congress wished to do so. In this view, any modification of the exemption by the Congress would be the use of a "control" which it has been exercising since the enactment of the income tax in 1913. Others felt that the exemption feature has its roots in the separation of powers doctrine set forth in the Constitution and that removal of the exemption involves a basic change in this doctrine requiring a constitutional amendment. Since the constitutional issue was ruled out of order at the beginning of the conference, this aspect of the controversy was dropped without further discussion. But the question whether exemption removal would mean more federal control in practice was admissible and was discussed at length.

One group stated that removal of the exemption would almost certainly result in considerably more federal control over state-local fiscal affairs. Some felt that it would be a first step toward eliminating the federal system and cited the experience in Australia as evidence. It was alleged that removal of the exemption feature in Australia in the 1940's was followed by other steps which reduced the fiscal powers of the states and marked "the end of the federal era in the constitutional relations of the commonwealth states" (a quotation attributed to Prime Minister Menzies). Others added that some Canadian municipalities were having so much difficulty in marketing their debt that observers there were suggesting the adoption of the exemption feature to preserve fiscal independence for local government.

Even the *possibility* of more federal control was regarded by some of the participants as sufficient argument against removal. In this view, inefficiencies or tax inequities arising from the exemption feature are trivial as compared to the dangers of more centralization of fiscal activity. Moreover, they pointed out that there are many other inequities in the federal tax system and stated that the tax exemption of state-local securities should not be singled out for special attention.

Those expressing concern about federal control opposed any alternative method of compensation by legislative action on the ground that it is impossible to guarantee that future Congresses will not tamper with the initial arrangements. They further felt that no alternative compensation could be devised that in practice would (1) compensate each state and local borrowing unit exactly for its higher borrowing costs; and (2) guarantee that the value of the compensation would be equivalent to the value of the exemption in future years. Some stated that an alternative subsidy might encourage too much state-local borrowing and poor borrowing practices. After some discussion, this point was qualified. It was agreed that, if the alternative compensation just offset the rise in interest costs to each locality, the volume of borrowing would not be affected. However, it was argued that there might be a more liberal settlement and that this would encourage unnecessary borrowing.

A number of participants took issue with the views just summarized. They argued that efficiency and tax equity were important enough to justify exploring the possibility of substituting for the tax exemption an alternative formula which would not involve any greater degree of federal control. (Some expressed disapproval of any form of compensation, but agreed that it was probably a political necessity.) In their view, the fear of a significant increase in federal control over the activities of the states and localities was entirely emotional. In general, this group was receptive to any one of a number of "automatic" formulas, such as a fixed proportion of the interest costs returned to states and localities or, if this were not acceptable, a tax credit for bondholders. Although these alternatives would not ensure a quid pro quo for each borrowing unit, they felt that there was nothing sacrosanct about the division of compensation implicit in the present exemption feature. They also expressed the opinion that most alternatives would probably ultimately overcompensate for the tax exemption, because they expect the interest rate differential between taxable and tax-exempt securities to decline in the future.

These participants did not accept the view that a change in the tax exemption required the adoption of a constitutional amendment. They were more confident in the ability and willingness of future Congresses to avoid intruding into areas of fiscal responsibility currently occupied by the states and localities. And they rejected the argument that the exemption should not be touched because it is only one of many inequities in the tax system; such a position, they pointed out, merely highlights the need for general tax reform, which, they agreed, is long overdue.

At one point in the discussion, there seemed to be a measure of agreement among a sizable number of the participants that the interests of both federal and local government might be better served by a method of assistance that would be more valuable to the states and municipalities than the tax exemption on their bonds and would also be entirely free of federal control. But this agreement was upset by the diversion of the discussion to consideration of the possibility that the federal government might wish to have a voice in how its revenue would be used. In the view of those inclined in this direction, the exemption feature is a subsidy and should be acknowledged as such; hence, what is needed is not some automatic alternative, but a program of direct federal support for state-local outlays rather than borrowing. This position was challenged by those who defended the exemption on political grounds, and it also drew dissents from several of the participants who had favored removal of the exemption on equity and efficiency grounds. As the conference ended, it became clear that many of those present would not support modification of the exemption unless an alternative method of compensation could be devised which would not involve any federal participation, let alone interference, in the purposes for which state-local borrowing is undertaken.

List of Conference Participants

Jeff B. Bates
  State Treasurer
  South Carolina

William R. Biggs
  Vice President
  The Bank of New York

Harvey E. Brazer
  Deputy Assistant Secretary
  U. S. Treasury

Beverly Briley
  County Manager,
  Davidson County
  Tennessee

Bernhard G. Bechhoefer
  Attorney
  Scharfeld, Segal, Baron &
    Stambler

Robert D. Calkins
  President
  The Brookings Institution

Joseph Clark
  Managing Director
  Municipal Finance Officers
    Association

Walter W. Craigie
  F. W. Craigie & Company

E. Lynn Crossley
  Auditor
  Dallas, Texas

John W. de Milhau
  Vice President
  The Chase Manhattan Bank

* Deceased August 13, 1962.

L. Laszlo Ecker-Racz
  Assistant Director
  Advisory Commission on Inter-
    governmental Relations

D. M. Ellinwood
  Vice President
  Moody's Investors Service

Daniel Goldberg
  General Solicitor
  Port of New York Authority

Raymond Goldsmith
  Professor of Economics
  Yale University

Raymond Hengren
  Assistant Chief
  Division of Research & Statistics
  Federal Deposit Insurance Cor-
    poration

Cushman McGee*
  Partner
  R. W. Pressprich & Co.

Allan H. Meltzer
  Professor of Economics
  Graduate School of Industrial
    Administration
  Carnegie Institute of Technology

Frank E. Morris
  Deputy Assistant to the Secre-
    tary
  U. S. Treasury Department

William S. Morris
  William S. Morris & Co.

127

Conference Participants *(Continued)*

James Mitchell
  Director
  Advanced Study Program
  The Brookings Institution

Roger F. Murray
  Professor of Economics
  Columbia University

Arthur Naftalin
  Mayor of Minneapolis

David J. Ott
  Assistant Professor of Economics
  Southern Methodist University

Donald C. Patterson
  Vice President
  Chemical Bank
  New York Trust Co.

Joseph A. Pechman
  Director of Economic Studies
  The Brookings Institution

D. K. Pfeffer
  Senior Vice President
  First National City Bank (N.Y.)

Roland I. Robinson
  Professor of Economics
  Michigan State University

Lawrence H. Seltzer
  Professor of Economics
  Wayne State University

Frank P. Smeal
  Vice President
  Morgan Guaranty Trust
  Company

Dan Throop Smith
  Professor of Finance
  Harvard Business School

Warren Smith
  Professor of Economics
  University of Michigan

Stanley S. Surrey
  Assistant Secretary
  U. S. Treasury

John F. Thompson
  Scudder, Stevens and Clark

Walter H. Tyler
  Standard and Poor's Corp.

APPENDIX TABLES

TABLE A–1. State and Local Government Securities Outstanding and Distribution among Holders, 1900–1960

(End of calendar year; billions of dollars)

Year		Amount Held By:							
	Total Out- standing	Com- mercial Banks	Life Insurance Companies	Mutual Savings Banks	Other Insurance Companies	Federal Govern- ment	State and Local Govern- ment	Indi- viduals	All Others
	(1)	(2)	(3)	(4)	(5)	(6)	(7)	(8)	(9)
1900	2.0	0.2	0.1	0.6	0.1	—	0.5	0.5	—
01	2.1	0.2	0.1	0.6	0.1	—	0.5	0.6	—
02	2.2	0.2	0.1	0.6	0.1	—	0.6	0.6	—
03	2.3	0.2	0.1	0.7	0.1	—	0.6	0.6	—
04	2.5	0.3	0.1	0.7	0.1	—	0.6	0.7	—
1905	2.6	0.3	0.1	0.7	0.1	—	0.7	0.7	—
06	2.7	0.3	0.1	0.7	0.1	—	0.7	0.8	—
07	3.0	0.4	0.1	0.7	0.1	—	0.8	0.9	—
08	3.3	0.4	0.2	0.7	0.1	—	0.8	1.1	—
09	3.5	0.4	0.2	0.7	0.2	—	0.9	1.1	—
1910	3.8	0.4	0.2	0.8	0.2	—	1.0	1.2	—
11	4.1	0.5	0.2	0.8	0.2	—	1.1	1.3	—
12	4.4	0.5	0.2	0.8	0.2	—	1.1	1.6	—
13	4.5	0.5	0.2	0.8	0.2	—	1.1	1.7	—
14	5.0	0.7	0.2	0.9	0.2	—	1.2	1.8	—
1915	5.5	0.7	0.3	0.8	0.3	—	1.3	2.1	—
16	5.9	0.8	0.3	0.9	0.3	—	1.4	2.2	—
17	6.3	0.9	0.3	0.8	0.3	—	1.4	2.6	—
18	6.7	0.9	0.3	0.7	0.3	—	1.4	3.1	—
19	7.1	1.0	0.3	0.7	0.4	—	1.7	3.0	—
1920	8.1	1.0	0.3	0.7	0.4	—	1.9	3.8	—
21	9.2	1.0	0.4	0.7	0.5	—	2.0	4.6	—
22	10.4	1.1	0.4	0.7	0.5	—	2.3	5.4	—
23	11.4	1.2	0.4	0.7	0.6	—	2.5	6.0	—
24	12.2	1.4	0.4	0.7	0.6	—	2.7	6.4	—
1925	13.0	1.5	0.4	0.8	0.7	—	2.9	6.7	—
26	13.8	1.7	0.4	0.8	0.8	—	3.2	6.9	—
27	14.8	1.8	0.4	0.9	0.8	—	3.5	7.4	—
28	15.8	2.0	0.5	0.9	0.9	—	3.7	7.8	—
29	16.9	2.1	0.6	0.9	0.9	—	4.0	8.4	—
1930	18.1	2.4	0.7	1.0	0.9	—	4.2	8.9	—
31	19.4	2.2	0.8	1.0	0.9	—	3.6	10.9	—
32	19.6	2.4	0.9	1.0	0.8	—	3.5	10.1	—
33	19.5	2.3	1.0	0.9	0.8	0.1	3.6	10.8	—
34	19.3	2.6	1.2	0.9	0.8	0.1	3.8	9.9	—
1935	19.7	2.8	1.4	0.8	0.8	0.2	3.9	9.8	—
36	19.8	2.8	1.6	0.8	0.8	0.2	4.0	9.6	—
37	19.6	2.7	1.7	0.8	0.8	0.2	4.0	9.4	—
38	19.9	3.1	1.7	0.7	0.8	0.5	4.0	8.8	0.3
39	20.3	3.4	1.9	0.6	0.8	0.5	3.9	8.5	0.7
1940	20.8	3.7	2.1	0.6	0.8	0.6	3.9	8.1	1.0
41	20.7	3.7	2.0	0.4	0.9	0.7	3.9	8.0	1.1
42	19.9	3.6	1.8	0.3	0.9	0.7	3.8	7.7	1.1
43	18.7	3.3	1.5	0.2	0.9	0.6	3.6	7.5	1.1
44	17.5	3.5	1.1	0.1	0.7	0.5	3.2	7.4	1.0

TABLE A–1. (Continued)

Year	Total Outstanding	Commercial Banks	Life Insurance Companies	Mutual Savings Banks	Other Insurance Companies	Federal Government	State and Local Government	Individuals	All Others
					Amount Held By:				
	(1)	(2)	(3)	(4)	(5)	(6)	(7)	(8)	(9)
1945	16.8	4.0	0.7	0.1	0.6	0.5	2.6	7.2	1.1
46	19.8	4.4	0.6	0.1	0.6	0.3	2.4	10.9	0.3
47	21.2	5.3	0.6	0.1	0.6	0.5	2.5	11.4	0.2
48	23.4	5.7	0.9	0.1	0.9	0.6	2.6	12.4	0.2
49	25.7	6.5	1.1	0.1	1.2	0.5	3.1	12.9	0.3
1950	28.8	8.1	1.2	0.1	1.4	0.6	3.6	13.4	0.4
51	31.1	9.2	1.2	0.1	1.7	0.8	3.8	13.8	0.5
52	34.3	10.2	1.2	0.3	2.1	1.1	4.0	15.0	0.4
53	37.8	10.8	1.3	0.4	2.9	0.8	4.4	16.8	0.4
54	42.0	12.6	1.8	0.6	3.6	0.5	4.7	17.8	0.4
1955	45.4	12.7	2.0	0.6	4.3	0.5	5.1	19.9	0.3
56	48.7	12.9	2.3	0.7	5.0	0.6	5.6	21.6	0.1
57	53.6	13.9	2.4	0.7	5.6	0.8	6.0	23.9	0.3
58	59.5	16.5	2.7	0.7	6.3	1.0	6.5	25.4	0.4
59	64.9	17.0	3.2	0.7	7.2	1.2	7.0	28.3	0.3
1960[a]	68.5	17.6	3.6	0.7	8.5	1.6	7.2	29.9	—

Sources:

Col. (1) Total outstanding; 1900–45, Raymond A. Goldsmith, *A Study of Saving in the United States* (National Bureau of Economic Research, 1955) Vol. 1, Table G-21, p. 1077. Figures obtained by adding the state government debt figure of col. (1) (after it has been converted from end of fiscal year to end of calendar year by taking the arithmetic average of the fiscal year and the one following it) to the local debt figure, col. (2). From 1933 to 1945 add Federal Government holdings, col. (6), to this sum. 1946–59, *Federal Reserve Bulletin* (August 1960), p. 943, Table 8F, line (S), credit market instruments. From 1946 on, the *Bulletin* data are not directly comparable to earlier Goldsmith estimates.

Col. (2) Commercial Banks; 1900–37, Goldsmith, *op. cit.*, Table V-74, col. 4, p. 577; 1938–46, Board of Governors, Federal Reserve System, *Flow of Funds in the United States, 1939–1953*, p. 344, Table 78-B, line (f); 1947–59, *Federal Reserve Bulletin*, August 1960, Table 8, line (M), p. 944.

Col. (3) Life Insurance Companies; 1900–37, Goldsmith op. *cit.*, Table I-6, col. 2, p. 456, estimates raised by multiplying 1.123 to link FRB data for later years, 1.123 being twelve years (1938–49) average ratio of Goldsmith—FRB estimates, 1938–47, FOF Table 78-B, line (i); 1948–60 from Institute of Life Insurance, *Life Insurance Fact Book*, 1960, p. 69.

Col. (4) Mutual Savings Banks, 1900–37, Goldsmith op. *cit.*, Table L-29, col. 8, p. 415; 1938–46, FOF, Table 78-B, line (g); 1947–59, *Federal Reserve Bulletin*, August 1960, Table 8-H.1, line (H).

Col. (5) Other Insurance Companies; 1900–37, sums of (1) Fraternal Orders (Goldsmith, op. *cit.*, Table I-10, Col. 8, p. 462), (2) Mutual accident, (Goldsmith, Table I-14, col. 6, p. 467), (3) Fire and Marine Insurance (V-55, col. 7, p. 553) and (4) Casualty and Miscellaneous (V-56, col. 7, p. 555); 1938–45, FOF, Table 78-B; line (j); 1946–59 difference of total insurance sector (*Federal Reserve Bulletin*, August 1960, Table 8-H.2, line G) and life insurance companies.

Col. (6) Federal Government; 1933–37, Goldsmith, Table F-14, col. 4, p. 998, December figures; 1938–45, FOF, Table 78-B, line (d); 1946–59, *Federal Reserve Bulletin* (August 1960), Table 8-F, line (T), other loans.

Col. (7) State and Local Government; 1900–37, derived by summing the following Goldsmith estimates: A) State government, Table G-17, col. (3) and (4) converted to year-end base as in the Total Outstanding column, B) Local government, Table G-8, col. (3) and (4), p. 1057. Sum then adjusted by multplying .967 to link with FRB data for later years. .967 is 12 year average ratio for Goldsmith-FRB estimates. 1938–45, FOF, Table 78-B, line (m); 1946–59, *Federal Reserve Bulletin* (August 1960), Table 8-F, line (Q), p. 943.

Col. (8) Individuals, 1900–37 holdings are residuals between total securities outstanding and nonindividuals holdings; 1938–45, FOF, Table 78-B, line (b); 1946–59, *Federal Reserve Bulletin* (August 1960), p. 941. Table 8-A, line (e) consumers and nonprofit organization (nonprofit organization holdings are negligible). From 1946 on, data are not directly comparable with that of earlier years.

Col. (9) Residual.

[a] Preliminary.

TABLE A–2. FHA Series on Monthly Averages of Friday Yields of Recently Issued Aaa to Baa Corporate Bonds (Moody-rated), 1951–1961

(Percent)

Month	1951	1952	1953	1954	1955	1956	1957	1958	1959	1960	1961
					Aaa						
January	2.68	3.09	3.11	3.23	2.99	3.20	4.08	4.07	4.48	5.11	4.62
February	2.70	3.07	3.17	3.20	3.06	3.16	4.13	3.98	4.42	5.01	4.47
March	2.82	3.06	—ᵃ	3.16	3.09	3.21	4.19	3.91	4.37	4.96	4.32
April	2.92	3.06	—ᵃ	3.13	3.08	3.39	4.19	3.79	4.40	4.93	4.45
May	3.04	3.14	3.68	3.08	3.11	3.40	4.24	3.77	4.60	4.89	4.52
June	3.12	3.13	3.72	3.02	3.16	3.46	4.52	3.80	4.71	4.80	4.67
July	3.07	3.13	3.62	2.98	3.21	3.51	4.55	3.94	—ᵃ	4.71	4.70
August	3.02	3.10	3.60	2.97	3.23	3.72	4.61	4.19	4.85	4.55	4.62
September	2.99	3.10	3.57	3.00	3.20	3.76	4.58	4.31	4.92	4.62	4.56
October	3.02	3.11	3.42	2.97	3.19	3.77	4.77	4.26	4.95	4.65	
November	3.08	3.08	3.37	2.97	3.18	3.89	4.67	4.34	5.14	4.69	
December	3.10	3.06	3.30	2.97	3.23	4.06	4.23	4.44	5.16	4.72	
					Aa						
January	2.70	3.18	3.27	3.20	3.05	3.21	4.19	4.28	4.48	5.09	4.69
February	2.73	3.11	3.32	3.13	3.13	3.15	4.28	3.84	4.48	4.96	4.50
March	2.91	3.16	3.34	2.99	3.16	3.22	4.31	4.01	4.41	4.93	4.38
April	3.01	3.17	3.45	3.01	3.15	3.45	4.31	3.92	4.48	4.85	4.50
May	2.99	3.17	3.67	3.00	3.18	3.50	4.34	3.88	4.64	4.90	4.55
June	3.07	3.18	3.84	3.03	3.20	3.54	4.64	3.85	4.77	4.85	4.67
July	3.09	3.20	3.71	3.01	3.21	3.61	4.75	3.94	4.73	4.73	4.68
August	3.01	3.20	3.66	3.00	3.26	3.81	4.75	4.15	4.76	4.60	4.67
September	2.99	3.18	3.69	3.03	3.29	3.88	4.74	4.42	5.04	4.61	4.62
October	2.97	3.18	3.48	3.01	3.26	3.88	4.79	4.39	5.07	4.64	
November	3.19	3.12	3.38	3.00	3.20	3.91	4.76	4.31	5.08	4.67	
December	3.23	3.12	3.30	3.00	3.24	4.06	4.40	4.40	5.16	4.78	
					A						
January	2.93	3.39	3.37	3.40	3.14	3.39	4.50	4.36	4.62	5.04	4.79
February	2.90	3.32	3.45	3.30	3.18	3.33	4.41	4.04	4.47	5.03	4.52
March	3.03	3.31	3.57	3.14	3.20	3.36	4.43	4.14	4.47	4.87	4.51
April	3.15	3.22	3.67	3.13	3.18	3.56	4.49	4.08	4.64	4.95	4.62
May	3.16	3.31	3.85	3.16	3.32	3.55	4.63	4.04	4.75	5.09	4.71
June	3.27	3.51	4.01	3.13	3.32	3.60	5.06	4.06	4.91	5.06	4.95
July	3.32	3.40	3.89	3.14	3.28	3.68	5.12	4.13	4.96	4.93	4.86
August	3.32	3.30	3.84	3.15	3.34	3.85	5.03	4.41	5.02	4.70	4.82
September	3.28	3.37	3.86	3.22	3.44	4.18	4.88	4.61	5.22	4.68	4.75
October	3.35	3.41	3.78	3.20	3.49	4.30	4.91	4.86	5.27	4.77	
November	3.43	3.33	3.59	3.07	3.41	4.32	4.99	4.68	5.37	4.91	
December	3.49	3.32	3.53	3.10	3.46	4.34	4.64	4.58	5.26	4.78	

TABLE A–2. (Continued).

Month	1951	1952	1953	1954	1955	1956	1957	1958	1959	1960	1961
					Baa						
January	—ᵃ	—ᵃ	—ᵃ	4.05	3.75	—ᵃ	5.22	4.90	4.98	5.31	4.95
February	—ᵃ	—ᵃ	—ᵃ	3.96	—ᵃ	5.23	5.11	4.36	4.83	5.71	4.75
March	—ᵃ	—ᵃ	3.82	3.94	—ᵃ	4.76	5.16	4.88	4.70	5.64	4.71
April	—ᵃ	—ᵃ	3.87	3.82	3.91	5.05	4.71	4.93	5.11	5.51	5.06
May	—ᵃ	3.91	3.99	3.53	3.91	5.10	5.18	4.71	5.14	5.30	5.05
June	—ᵃ	4.02	4.03	3.35	3.86	—ᵃ	5.34	4.62	5.17	5.40	5.21
July	—ᵃ	4.28	3.99	3.35	3.69	4.82	5.67	4.58	5.04	5.38	5.18
August	—ᵃ	4.28	—ᵃ	—ᵃ	3.67	5.01	5.78	4.64	5.11	5.15	5.16
September	—ᵃ	4.28	4.60	3.35	3.61	5.07	5.70	4.79	5.38	5.10	5.06
October	—ᵃ	4.16	4.22	3.44	3.45	5.02	5.65	5.01	5.22	5.11	
November	—ᵃ	3.95	3.98	3.82	—ᵃ	5.05	5.60	5.21	5.19	—ᵃ	
December	—ᵃ	—ᵃ	4.07	3.78	—ᵃ	5.09	5.37	5.11	5.24	—ᵃ	

Source: Federal Housing Administration. Yields computed by the Federal Housing Administration from quotations on recent issues of corporate bonds selected from those listed in the weekly statistical edition of the *Commericial and Financial Chronicle* in a section entitled "Recent Security & Convertible Debenture Issues."

ᵃ No data available.

TABLE A–3. IBA Series on New Issue Yields on State and Local Government Securities, 1957–1961, Monthly

(Percent per annum)

Year and Month	Aaa			Aa			A			Baa			Average of Medians Top Four Grades		
	5 Years[a]	10 Years[a]	20 Years	5 Years[a]	10 Years[a]	20 Years	5 Years[a]	10 Years[a]	20 Years	5 Years[a]	10 Years[a]	20 Years	5 Years[a]	10 Years[a]	20 Years
1957															
January			2.73			2.83			3.40			3.95			3.23
February			2.60			2.85			3.30			3.65			3.10
March			2.80			3.00			3.40			3.85			3.26
April			2.80			3.00			3.40			3.83			3.26
May			3.05			3.20			3.60			3.95			3.45
June			3.15			3.55			3.85			4.25			3.70
July			3.15			3.30			3.80			4.18			3.61
August			3.30			3.60			4.03			4.33			3.82
September			3.15			3.50			3.95			4.30			3.73
October			3.10			3.30			3.70			4.20			3.58
November			3.00			3.23			3.60			3.95			3.45
December			2.70			2.78			3.25			3.70			3.11
Average			2.96			3.18			3.61			4.01			3.44
1958															
January	2.00	2.15	2.45	2.10	2.40	2.70	2.40	2.75	3.10	2.73	3.20	3.60	2.31	2.63	2.96
February	1.90	2.20	2.63	2.00	2.40	2.88	2.28	2.75	3.25	2.60	3.10	3.65	2.20	2.61	3.11
March	1.75	2.25	2.70	2.00	2.50	2.90	2.15	2.70	3.40	2.55	3.10	3.65	2.11	2.64	3.16
April	1.60	2.20	2.70	1.70	2.30	2.75	2.00	2.55	3.18	2.20	2.93	3.60	1.88	2.50	3.06
May	1.60	2.25	2.65	1.75	2.30	2.80	1.90	2.50	3.10	2.23	2.90	3.50	1.91	2.49	3.01
June	1.70	2.30	2.73	1.80	2.40	2.90	2.00	2.60	3.25	2.15	2.80	3.50	2.03	2.53	3.10
July	1.80	2.40	2.88	1.90	2.50	3.10	2.10	2.75	3.30	2.30	2.90	3.60	2.30	2.64	3.22
August	1.90	2.50	3.05	2.20	2.85	3.40	2.40	3.10	3.75	2.68	3.38	3.95	2.64	2.96	3.54
September	2.30	2.75	3.10	2.40	2.90	3.45	2.75	3.33	3.85	3.10	3.70	4.15	2.71	3.17	3.64
October	2.30	2.75	3.00	2.58	3.00	3.30	2.85	3.25	3.68	3.10	3.63	4.00	2.61	3.16	3.50
November	2.28	2.68	2.95	2.50	2.85	3.20	2.68	3.10	3.50	2.98	3.43	3.85	2.55	3.02	3.38
December	2.25	2.68	3.00	2.35	2.75	3.08	2.70	3.20	3.60	2.90	3.40	3.83	2.26	3.01	3.38
Average	1.95	2.43	2.82	2.11	2.60	3.04	2.35	2.88	3.41	2.63	3.21	3.74		2.78	3.25
1959															
January	2.35	2.75	3.10	2.50	2.90	3.20	2.80	3.20	3.60	3.00	3.53	4.00	2.66	3.10	3.48
February	2.40	2.80	3.13	2.50	2.90	3.23	2.60	3.05	3.48	2.90	3.35	3.83	2.60	3.03	3.42

March	2.35	2.75	3.08	2.45	2.85	3.15	2.60	3.00	3.40	2.90	3.30	3.80	2.58	2.98	3.36
April	2.40	2.80	3.00	2.55	2.98	3.33	2.75	3.15	3.58	2.90	3.35	3.90	2.65	3.07	3.45
May	2.63	2.93	3.25	2.80	3.10	3.50	3.00	3.40	3.85	3.15	3.70	4.10	2.90	3.28	3.66
June	2.80	3.10	3.38	2.98	3.25	3.65	3.10	3.50	3.90	3.40	3.90	4.25	3.07	3.44	3.80
July	2.85	3.08	3.40	3.00	3.30	3.63	3.15	3.60	3.95	3.38	3.95	4.20	3.10	3.50	3.80
August	2.83	3.08	3.30	2.93	3.25	3.52	3.10	3.50	3.80	3.20	3.70	4.05	3.02	3.38	3.68
September	3.10	3.30	3.63	3.18	3.43	3.75	3.40	3.75	4.07	3.65	4.03	4.40	3.33	3.63	3.96
October	2.90	3.05	3.35	3.10	3.20	3.45	3.30	3.55	3.80	3.50	3.90	4.15	3.20	3.43	3.69
November	2.85	3.00	3.20	3.00	3.20	3.40	3.25	3.45	3.80	3.45	3.77	4.00	3.14	3.36	3.60
December	2.95	3.15	3.35	3.05	3.25	3.55	3.30	3.60	3.90	3.50	3.90	4.15	3.20	3.48	3.74
Average	2.70	2.99	3.26	2.84	3.13	3.45	3.03	3.40	3.76	3.24	3.70	4.07	2.95	3.31	3.64
1960															
January	2.98	3.18	3.38	3.15	3.35	3.65	3.50	3.80	4.10	3.70	4.05	4.30	3.33	3.60	3.86
February	2.90	3.05	3.50	3.03	3.25	3.45	3.30	3.50	3.85	3.50	3.90	4.25	3.18	3.43	3.76
March	2.90	3.05	3.30	3.00	3.23	3.45	3.20	3.45	3.73	3.40	3.90	4.18	3.13	3.41	3.67
April	2.80	2.95	3.20	2.95	3.15	3.43	3.18	3.45	3.75	3.38	3.80	4.10	3.08	3.34	3.62
May	2.80	3.05	3.30	2.90	3.15	3.40	3.20	3.50	3.78	3.40	3.80	4.10	3.08	3.38	3.65
June	2.70	2.95	3.20	2.80	3.10	3.35	3.05	3.40	3.60	3.30	3.75	4.05	2.96	3.30	3.55
July	2.57	2.88	3.15	2.70	3.00	3.40	3.00	3.45	3.75	3.30	3.75	4.00	2.89	3.27	3.58
August	2.20	2.60	2.95	2.30	2.80	3.15	2.55	3.25	3.50	2.90	3.40	3.80	2.49	3.01	3.35
September	2.25	2.75	3.10	2.30	2.80	3.30	2.60	3.10	3.60	2.88	3.38	3.83	2.51	3.01	3.46
October	2.33	2.83	3.23	2.45	2.95	3.35	2.60	3.15	3.70	3.00	3.50	3.95	2.60	3.11	3.56
November	2.10	2.60	3.00	2.30	2.80	3.20	2.45	3.00	3.55	2.75	3.35	3.85	2.40	2.94	3.40
December	2.15	2.65	3.08	2.30	2.80	3.25	2.45	3.00	3.60	2.73	3.35	3.88	2.41	2.95	3.45
Average	2.56	2.88	3.20	2.68	3.03	3.36	2.92	3.34	3.71	3.19	3.66	4.02	2.84	3.23	3.58
1961															
January	2.15	2.65	3.10	2.30	2.80	3.30	2.50	3.00	3.60	2.80	3.30	3.85	2.44	2.94	3.46
February	2.20	2.70	3.15	2.25	2.75	3.20	2.40	2.90	3.48	2.60	3.20	3.80	2.36	2.89	3.41
March	2.30	2.80	3.25	2.35	2.90	3.35	2.50	3.00	3.60	2.65	3.28	3.80	2.45	3.00	3.50
April	2.30	2.85	3.20	2.40	2.95	3.45	2.55	3.10	3.60	2.80	3.33	3.90	2.51	3.06	3.54
May	2.20	2.70	3.20	2.30	2.80	3.25	2.50	3.00	3.50	2.75	3.30	3.80	2.44	2.95	3.44
June	2.30	2.90	3.38	2.40	2.95	3.50	2.60	3.10	3.60	2.80	3.30	3.85	2.53	3.06	3.58
July	2.30	2.90	3.25	2.40	2.93	3.43	2.60	3.10	3.60	2.75	3.30	3.90	2.51	3.06	3.55
August	2.30	2.80	3.23	2.45	3.00	3.45	2.60	3.10	3.65	2.80	3.40	3.90	2.54	3.08	3.56
September	2.25	2.75	3.25	2.35	2.95	3.40	2.50	3.00	3.70	2.73	3.30	3.83	2.51	3.04	3.55
October	2.25	2.75	3.20	2.40	2.85	3.30	2.50	3.00	3.50	2.65	3.20	3.75	2.44	2.95	3.44
November	2.25	2.75	3.30	2.40	2.90	3.35	2.50	3.00	3.50	2.70	3.25	3.85	2.46	2.98	3.50
December	2.25	2.75	3.25	2.40	2.90	3.45	2.50	3.00	3.50	2.75	3.40	3.85	2.48	3.01	3.51
Average	2.25	2.78	3.23	2.37	2.89	3.37	2.53	3.03	3.57	2.73	3.30	3.84	2.47	3.00	3.50

Source: *IBA Statistical Bulletin*, various issues, 1957–1962.
ᵃ No data available for 1957.

TABLE A–4. Average Yields on New Commitments for Directly Placed Corporate Bonds, Reporting Life Insurance Companies, 1959–1961[a]

(Percent)

Month	Classified[b]	Unclassified	Total
1959			
September	5.68%	—[c]	—[c]
October	5.78	—[c]	—[c]
November	6.14	—[c]	—[c]
December	5.96	—[c]	—[c]
1960			
January	6.05	6.08%	6.05%
February	6.00	6.17	6.04
March	5.83	6.32	5.94
April	5.92	6.30	6.01
May	5.97	6.89	6.18
June	6.01	6.43	6.10
July	5.89	5.95	5.90
August	5.82	6.12	5.92
September	5.79	6.07	5.84
October	5.73	6.32	5.92
November	5.62	5.77	5.66
December	5.95	6.05	5.96
1961			
January	5.68	6.12	5.79
February	5.62	6.01	5.80
March	5.55	6.39	5.77
April	5.61	6.00	5.69

Source: Life Insurance Association of America.

[a] These data include single authorizations.

[b] Classified placements refer to those falling in the first four quality grades, as reported by participating companies. Unclassified placements are all other placements including those of a quality lower than fourth grade, convertible obligations, foreign corporates, oil production loans, and issues with which stocks or warrants are received.

[c] No data available.

TABLE A–5. Bond Yields in Canada, 1953–1961

(Monthly)

Date	Long Term Dominion	10 Municipal Bonds	10 Provincial Bonds	10 Public Utility Bonds	10 Industrial Bonds	40 Bond Average
1953						
January 1	3.59	4.60	4.15	4.33	4.43	4.38
February 2	3.60	4.60	4.16	4.34	4.41	4.38
March 2	3.64	4.64	4.11	4.35	4.44	4.39
April 2	3.65	4.65	4.13	4.35	4.42	4.39
May 1	3.67	4.66	4.13	4.38	4.48	4.41
June 3	3.70	4.68	4.16	4.37	4.47	4.42
July 3	3.70	4.69	4.16	4.40	4.56	4.45
August 4	3.73	4.70	4.18	4.41	4.55	4.46
September 1	3.76	4.73	4.20	4.41	4.54	4.47
October 1	3.76	4.72	4.17	4.38	4.56	4.46
November 2	3.69	4.66	4.15	4.33	4.55	4.42
December 1	3.65	4.58	4.09	4.32	4.52	4.38
1954						
January 4	3.61	4.50	4.07	4.31	4.48	4.34
February 1	3.54	4.49	4.05	4.31	4.44	4.32
March 1	3.41	4.36	3.98	4.25	4.38	4.24
April 1	3.06	4.02	3.57	4.06	4.16	3.95
May 3	3.04	3.92	3.45	3.89	4.07	3.83
June 1	3.05	3.81	3.38	3.86	4.06	3.78
June 29	3.02	3.78	3.40	3.83	4.05	3.76
August 4	2.98	3.79	3.38	3.80	4.02	3.75
September 1	2.97	3.77	3.36	3.77	4.02	3.73
October 1	2.94	3.77	3.34	3.73	4.01	3.71
November 1	2.94	3.76	3.32	3.75	4.02	3.71
December 1	2.95	3.77	3.33	3.76	4.01	3.72
1955						
January 3	2.96	3.75	3.34	3.75	4.00	3.71
February 1	2.95	3.75	3.36	3.75	4.00	3.71
March 1	2.85	3.74	3.32	3.74	3.97	3.69
April 1	2.82	3.66	3.29	3.73	3.97	3.66
May 2	2.88	3.66	3.27	3.69	3.97	3.65
June 1	2.89	3.66	3.28	3.69	3.93	3.64
June 30	2.89	3.65	3.27	3.69	3.93	3.63
August 2	2.98	3.65	3.30	3.69	3.93	3.64
September 2	3.06	3.70	3.41	3.75	3.97	3.71
October 3	3.10	3.72	3.50	3.73	4.00	3.74
November 1	3.15	3.73	3.53	3.75	4.00	3.75
December 3	3.30	3.90	3.70	3.85	4.11	3.91

TABLE A–5. (Continued)

Date	Long Term Dominion	10 Municipal Bonds	10 Provincial Bonds	10 Public Utility Bonds	10 Industrial Bonds	40 Bond Average
1956						
January 3	3.39	4.04	3.82	3.98	4.15	4.00
February 1	3.28	4.02	3.74	3.95	4.10	3.95
March 1	3.26	4.01	3.65	3.86	4.10	3.91
April 3	3.38	4.10	3.77	3.94	4.21	4.00
May 1	3.54	4.56	4.10	4.13	4.39	4.30
June 1	3.51	4.52	4.05	4.19	4.44	4.30
July 3	3.40	4.45	3.91	4.19	4.44	4.25
August 1	3.63	4.59	4.12	4.22	4.54	4.37
August 31	3.78	4.81	4.41	4.33	4.70	4.56
October 1	3.88	5.19	4.71	4.69	4.89	4.87
November 1	3.93	5.21	4.61	4.92	5.13	4.97
December 3	3.97	5.37	4.99	5.01	5.21	5.15
December 31	4.00	5.45	5.03	4.98	5.22	5.17
1957						
February 1	4.19	5.41	5.03	5.11	5.21	5.19
March 1	4.03	5.38	4.89	5.08	5.14	5.12
April 1	3.96	5.38	4.88	5.13	5.27	5.16
May 1	4.00	5.48	4.96	5.15	5.30	5.22
June 1	4.22	5.53	5.02	5.17	5.38	5.27
July 2	4.27	5.61	5.11	5.21	5.37	5.32
August 1	4.30	5.62	5.15	5.24	5.41	5.35
September 1	4.43	5.73	5.18	5.42	5.77	5.52
October 1	4.35	5.77	5.15	5.50	5.72	5.53
November 1	4.02	5.66	5.10	5.36	5.58	5.42
December 2	3.82	5.21	4.74	5.13	5.19	5.07
1958						
January 1	3.79	5.12	4.60	5.03	5.04	4.95
February 1	3.84	5.04	4.60	4.88	5.03	4.89
March 1	3.93	5.05	4.58	4.84	4.96	4.86
April 1	3.95	5.02	4.54	4.82	4.78	4.79
May 1	3.87	5.03	4.46	4.85	4.88	4.81
June 1	3.83	4.98	4.47	4.81	4.88	4.79
July 1	3.94	5.17	4.59	4.81	4.88	4.86
August 1	3.96	5.17	4.72	4.87	4.96	4.93
September 1	4.15	5.17	4.79	4.91	5.01	4.97
October 1	4.13	5.30	4.97	4.95	5.15	5.09
November 1	4.31	5.28	5.02	4.96	5.09	5.09
December 1	4.42	5.27	5.08	5.02	5.12	5.12

Date	Long Term Dominion	10 Municipal Bonds	10 Provincial Bonds	10 Public Utility Bonds	10 Industrial Bonds	40 Bond Average
1959						
January 1	4.48	5.38	5.14	5.14	5.22	5.22
February 1	4.53	5.41	5.18	5.14	5.17	5.23
March 1	4.65	5.52	5.17	5.17	5.17	5.26
April 1	4.80	5.52	5.22	5.20	5.20	5.29
May 1	4.88	5.55	5.23	5.20	5.25	5.31
June 1	4.94	5.71	5.39	5.47	5.42	5.50
July 1	4.94	5.84	5.52	5.47	5.63	5.61
August 1	4.97	5.86	5.61	5.57	5.60	5.66
September 1	5.29	6.20	5.97	5.78	5.78	5.93
October 1	5.80	6.60	6.19	6.01	6.05	6.21
November 1	5.45	6.53	6.06	6.00	6.03	6.15
December 1	5.58	6.52	5.97	6.00	6.02	6.13
1960						
January 1	5.70	6.60	6.12	6.04	6.14	6.23
February 1	5.87	6.60	6.19	6.17	6.22	6.30
March 1	5.63	6.56	6.05	6.14	6.20	6.24
April 1	5.43	6.24	5.79	6.02	6.00	6.01
May 1	5.34	6.06	5.74	5.93	5.91	5.91
June 1	5.22	6.06	5.73	5.83	5.82	5.86
July 1	5.13	5.88	5.54	5.58	5.56	5.64
August 1	5.21	5.84	5.51	5.50	5.52	5.59
September 1	4.82	5.67	5.32	5.37	5.33	5.42
October 1	4.77	5.61	5.28	5.29	5.24	5.35
November 1	4.92	5.60	5.40	5.38	5.39	5.44
December 1	5.35	5.95	5.60	5.54	5.62	5.68
1961						
January 1	5.38	5.97	5.68	5.45	5.61	5.68
February 1	5.26	5.94	5.70	5.49	5.62	5.69
March 1	5.13	5.83	5.53	5.47	5.51	5.59
March 30	5.26	5.85	5.65	5.51	5.61	5.66
May 1	5.31	5.92	5.74	5.54	5.68	5.72
June 1	5.21	5.82	5.62	5.48	5.60	5.63
June 30	4.98	5.71	5.37	5.37	5.47	5.48

Source: McCleod, Young, Weir & Co., Ltd.

INDEX